PEN

SIMPLE VE

Rosamond Richardson has
including a series for Sainsbury's. She also writes about the
countryside, and is the author of *Country Harvest* and *Swanbrooke
Down: A Century of Change in an English Village*. Rosamond has
presented several TV programmes for BBC 2, and has broadcast
regularly on BBC local radio. Her book *Seasonal Pleasures* was
published by Viking in 1990. She has three children and lives in
a small village in Essex.

SIMPLE VEGETARIAN MEALS

RECIPES FOR ONE AND TWO

ROSAMOND RICHARDSON

ILLUSTRATIONS BY AMANDA HALL

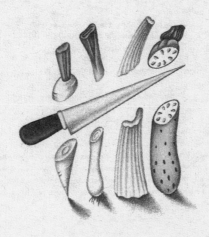

PENGUIN BOOKS

For 'M.B.'
with thanks for the idea

PENGUIN BOOKS

Published by the Penguin Group
Penguin Books Ltd, 27 Wrights Lane, London W8 5TZ, England
Penguin Books USA Inc., 375 Hudson Street, New York, New York 10014, USA
Penguin Books Australia Ltd, Ringwood, Victoria, Australia
Penguin Books Canada Ltd, 10 Alcorn Avenue, Toronto, Ontario, Canada M4V 5B2
Penguin Books (NZ) Ltd, 182–190 Wairau Road, Auckland 10, New Zealand

Penguin Books Ltd, Registered Offices: Harmondsworth, Middlesex, England

First published 1991
1 3 5 7 9 10 8 6 4 2

The moral right of the author and illustrator has been asserted

Printed in England by Clays Ltd, St Ives plc
Set in Monophoto Garamond

CONTENTS

INTRODUCTION

Cooking with flair does not have to be either complicated or expensive. Nor does cooking for small numbers have to be monotonous. You can devise memorable, healthy vegetarian meals that are both simple and inexpensive, using the wonderful variety of fresh foods now available in the shops.

You can make simple, daily vegetarian meals interesting, original and varied. Certainly cooking for one or two can present problems of monotony or expense, of effort entailed or time spent; and of what to do with leftovers. But although simplicity is the keynote of this style of cooking, it is a simplicity that does not exclude varied and interesting recipes from around the world, with all their delicious flavours. Vegetarian food lends itself comfortably to the brief of cooking economically, and with a certain style, for one or two people.

Eating alone, or *à deux*, does not have to be repetitious – which is one of the hazards of buying pre-cooked food. Although there are some excellent 'instant' and chilled pre-cooked meals available, quite a lot of them are not very exciting or particularly delicious, nor very varied. They are also relatively more expensive. In any case, the small print on the label may include ingredients that you would not choose to add to your home-cooking . . .

You may lead a busy working life with a minimum of time, money and energy to spend on cooking. This book is for you. You may be a student living away from home for the first time; or a young couple setting up house. You may be elderly and alone – or elderly and not alone! At whatever age, you may be living on your own from choice or not from choice: the insidious habits of eating alone – grabbing a piece of cheese and eating it standing up being typical of these – can become a thing of the past.

Added to economy, simplicity and speed is another important aspect: healthy eating. Cooking vegetarian food for one or two offers the possibility of selecting fresh, wholesome ingredients and deciding whether or not to use organically grown produce. Most of the recipes in the book have an eye to a low fat content, and none of the desserts is over-sweet or too rich. The beauty of natural flavours is the essence of this simple cookery.

People who eat on their own, or who regularly cook for two, need to be especially careful to maintain a nutritional balance in their diet. General guidelines agreed by nutritionists are to watch fats and sugars, keeping saturated fats down to 10 per cent of the daily intake, and unsaturated to 20 per cent. Sugar should amount to no more than 7 per cent. High-fibre carbohydrates should take pride of place at 40–50 per cent of the daily diet, and protein 11–15 per cent. Vegetarians get their protein from cheese, yogurt and dairy products, brown bread, rice and all the pulses. Many vegetables are high in protein too, as well as containing numerous vitamins and minerals, so eating good amounts of lightly cooked or raw vegetables is a simple way towards ensuring that you are eating a healthy diet.

A note on equipment: for ease and speed, a liquidizer or food-processor is a boon. Nowadays you can buy liquidizers for very little money, and you will find that you cover your costs very quickly – making wonderful soups or seasonal vegetable purées, for example, which will provide you with satisfying and nutritious food at low cost. I recently made a carrot and orange soup using my blender, with just a vegetable stock cube, the cooking juices from the carrots plus the orange juice: and it was sublime. The cost was ridiculously low! The convenience of making breadcrumbs, or puréeing pâtés and dips, is also well worth this small investment.

Secondly, I have to recommend a microwave oven, if at all possible. Vegetables steamed in a microwave retain all their flavour and texture; they are cooked in a matter of a few minutes; and there is minimal washing up because you serve them straight from the dish. Time-saving, labour-saving, no chores. A microwave oven is the solution to the 'can't be bothered' syndrome which is one of the curses of eating alone or cooking for two. Another bonus: reheating food in a microwave is brilliant: even yesterday's risotto emerges moist, light and full of flavour – and really hot! The same applies to soups, gratins and even cups of tea. A real bonus for the busy, the weary or the preoccupied . . .

Leftovers are very much a part of this scenario. Often it is difficult to keep the quantity of an interesting recipe down to two servings – usually it will feed three or even four. Nor is there much point in making the effort to cook in tiny quantities. But no problem: there is advice on cooking with leftovers in this book that deals with this aspect of cooking very effectively. Also, since most of the recipes serve around two or three people, there is scope in all of them for inspired 'leftover' meals. Cooking with leftovers can be immensely creative, good fun, quick and satisfying – a meal in moments with virtually no labour involved.

The store cupboard

There are certain ways of stocking your larder that will facilitate using the speedy and economic simplicity of the recipes in this book:

◇ A range of interesting vinegars: as well as white-wine vinegar, try raspberry vinegar, tarragon vinegar, balsamic vinegar – all of which enhance salad dressings and other dishes

◇ Tahini paste and sesame seeds

◇ A range of oils: good-quality olive oil, sunflower oil and ground-nut oil (for stir-frying). Dark sesame oil is delicious in various oriental-style dishes and salad dressings

◇ Vegetable stock cubes

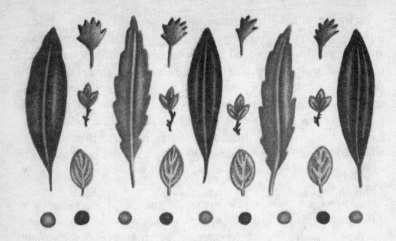

◇ Spices: garam masala powder and five-spice, from oriental grocers, as well as the classics – cinnamon, nutmeg, saffron, mace, cumin and coriander

◇ Good-quality dried mixed herbs (Provençal are wonderful)

◇ Soy sauce or tamari; black-bean sauce (from Chinese grocers)

◇ Mustards such as Dijon, moutarde de Meaux

◇ Crunchy peanut butter

◇ Rice: long-grain, short-grain, basmati, wild; rice-noodles

◇ Noodles: plain or egg (best bought from Chinese supermarkets)

◇ Pasta, e.g. twists, fettucine, linguini, spaghetti, etc.

◇ Pulses: lentils (red and green), chick peas, kidney beans, black-eyed beans, butterbeans, etc.

For the freezer

◇ Fresh root ginger, which can be grated on the fine side of the grater from frozen

◇ A supply of pesto sauce.

For the fridge

◇ A supply of thick Greek sheep's yogurt

◇ Mayonnaise

◇ Creamed coconut for some oriental sauces

◇ Parmesan.

In the garden, or in pots or a window box

◇ Fresh herbs: basil, coriander, dill, chives, parsley, marjoram and mint are among the most useful.

DIPS AND APPETIZERS

Blue Cheese Dip with Crudités

Serves 2

*Stilton, or other blue cheese,
40 g (1½ oz)*

½ a small onion, grated

*Natural yogurt, 100 g
(4 oz)*

Paprika to taste

*A selection of raw
vegetables*

Dips are wonderfully simple to prepare, and can be served as a snack before a meal, or as part of a salad table. This one, best made with Stilton, has a rich flavour that is beautifully balanced by the raw vegetables dipped into it.

Mash the blue cheese and mix it with the grated onion. Put into the blender with the yogurt and liquidize to a dipping consistency.

Season to taste with paprika and serve with sliced raw vegetables such as baby carrots, cucumber, cauliflower, courgettes, mushrooms, French beans and celery.

Zdadziki

Serves 2–3

½ a cucumber, peeled

Thick Greek yogurt,
100 g (4 oz)

1–2 cloves of garlic,
crushed

Mint, 1 tbs finely chopped

A classic Greek recipe, this dip of grated cucumber and thick yogurt is pungent with garlic, and fresh mint adds to its refreshing quality.

Grate the cucumber on the coarse side of the grater. Place it in a sieve and press the water out with the back of a spoon. Dry the grated cucumber on kitchen paper.

Then mix all the ingredients together and chill for at least 2 hours before serving. Serve with warm pitta bread.

Tahini Dip

Serves 2

1 large clove of garlic,
crushed

Juice of 1 lemon

Tahini, 5 tbs

Ground cumin, 1 tsp

Parsley, 2 tbs finely
chopped

Dark sesame oil to thin
out

Sesame seeds, 1 tbs
browned

1 hard-boiled egg, sliced, to
garnish

Salt to taste

This unusual dip has a strong, distinctive flavour reminiscent of Middle Eastern cookery – its source. It is delicious with pitta bread, and with florets of raw cauliflower to dip into it.

Blend the crushed garlic, lemon juice and tahini in the liquidizer until they make a smooth purée. Season with the cumin and add salt to taste. Stir in the parsley and mix well. Thin out to a dipping consistency with more sesame oil. Put into a serving-dish and sprinkle with the toasted sesame seeds. Put the slices of hard-boiled egg around the edge as a garnish.

Marinated Crudités Aïoli

Serves 2–3

For the marinade
*White wine and water,
300 ml (½ pint) each*

1 bay leaf

1 sprig thyme

Olive oil, 150 ml (¼ pint)

*Juice and grated rind of
1 lemon*

White-wine vinegar, 2 tbs

*4 coriander seeds and
4 peppercorns*

*½ a dried chilli, soaked in
warm water*

*Fresh root ginger, 15 g
(½ oz) peeled and grated*

1 clove of garlic, chopped

Salt

For the aïoli
*2 large cloves of garlic,
crushed*

*Mayonnaise, 300 ml
(½ pint)*

For the crudités
*Lightly steamed: baby
French beans, mange-tout,
broccoli florets, baby
sweetcorn, 750 g (1½ lb)
Raw: yellow peppers, baby
carrots, cauliflower florets,
button mushrooms*

For all its simplicity, aïoli always makes a memorable meal – thick, glossy mayonnaise, uncompromisingly garlicky, and aromatic vegetables to dip into it. Serve this with warm granary bread and the dish is complete.

Boil all the ingredients for the marinade together for 5 minutes. Pour over the prepared crudités and refrigerate for 24 hours.

To make the aïoli, stir the crushed garlic into the mayonnaise and mix well. Cover and leave to stand for at least an hour, preferably longer, before using.

Most of the vegetables used for the crudités can be eaten whole, but slice the peppers into thin strips before serving.

Peppers with Tarragon

Serves 2–3

1 red and 1 green pepper

1 large clove of garlic, chopped

Juice of 1 lemon

Tarragon, 2 tbs finely chopped

Salt and pepper

Olive oil, 3 tbs

Sprigs of tarragon to garnish

Skinned, grilled peppers in a garlic and tarragon dressing, arranged decoratively on a plate, make an elegant, light starter to a meal. Try using other coloured peppers, too – yellow, purple or white – to vary the effect.

Wash the peppers and cut into quarters. De-seed and remove the inedible parts. Grill the peppers for a few minutes, skin-side up. Leave to cool. Now remove the skin, which should peel away easily. Cut the peppers into strips.

Mix together the garlic, lemon juice, chopped tarragon, and some salt and pepper, and sprinkle over the peppers. Trickle the olive oil over the top and garnish with the sprigs of tarragon.

Grilled Melon with Cucumber

Per person

½ a round melon

¼ cucumber, peeled

Fresh summer herbs, 1 tbs finely chopped

Brown sugar, 2 tbs

A summery starter. Light and herby, this can be served either hot or cold. In the latter case the sugar will crystallize and harden, forming a coat over the fruit.

Scoop out the melon flesh with a 'baller'. Dice the cucumber into similar-sized pieces. Mix the herbs with the two fruits inside the melon shell. Sprinkle the brown sugar over the top, and leave under a hot grill until the sugar melts.

Avocado with Mushroom Filling

Serves 2

Button mushrooms, 175 g (6 oz) minced in the blender

Pesto sauce (see p. 120), 3 tbs

1 large ripe avocado, cut in half and stoned

Lettuce leaves to garnish

Mincing fresh raw mushrooms in the blender takes a few seconds only, and gives a better texture for this dish than chopping them by hand. Mixed with pesto sauce and heaped into the cavity of a ripe avocado, this makes a delectable starter.

Steam the minced mushrooms for 3 minutes. Cool, and drain off the juices. Mix the mushrooms with the pesto and place inside the hollow of the avocado halves. Place on a bed of lightly dressed lettuce leaves to serve (see pp. 121–3).

Grapefruit Cocktail

Serves 2

*½ a large grapefruit,
peeled and the pith removed*

*½ a large ripe avocado,
peeled, stoned and sliced*

*Seedless grapes, 75 g
(3 oz)*

*8 green olives, stoned and
halved (optional)*

*Cherry tomatoes, 75 g
(3 oz) skinned (see p. 67)
and quartered*

*Small bunch fresh lovage or
basil*

Natural yogurt, 3 tbs

*Garlic vinaigrette, 1 tbs
(see p. 122)*

Fresh, sharp flavours are the keynote of this appetizer: olives, tomatoes, grapes and avocado are balanced with the grapefruit and herbs in a yogurt dressing, and chilled. Summer food.

Divide the grapefruit into its segments and cut them into bite-sized pieces. Combine with the sliced avocado, grapes, optional olives and quartered tomatoes. Reserve a few of the basil or lovage leaves for garnish, slice the rest and mix them into the fruit. Finally mix the yogurt and vinaigrette, and dress the mixture. Pile into two individual glass dishes and chill. Serve garnished with the remaining leaves.

Celeriac Remoulade

Serves 2–3

*Celeriac, 225 g (8 oz)
peeled*

Mayonnaise, 5 tbs

*Gherkin and capers, 1 tbs
each finely chopped*

*'Fines herbes', 2 tbs finely
chopped*

A little mustard to taste

Classic French simplicity at its best, this celeriac salad is wonderful winter food. Serve it with fresh granary bread, either as a starter or for a light lunch with a tossed salad.

Cut the celeriac into thin strips, or grate it on the coarse side of the grater. Mix all the rest of the ingredients together and stir thoroughly into the celeriac. Put in a cool place for several hours before serving so that the flavours can amalgamate and the celeriac can soften in the sauce.

Avocado and Cream Cheese Dip

Serves 2–3

½ a large avocado, stoned

*Cooked spinach, 100 g
(4 oz) chopped*

*Low-fat curd cheese, 50 g
(2 oz) mashed*

1 clove of garlic, crushed

Lemon juice, 1–2 tsp

*2 spring onions, finely
chopped*

Salt and paprika

The mouthwatering texture of this rich green dip is the perfect base for its fresh, slightly garlicky flavour. A popular favourite for all times of the year.

Scoop the flesh out of the avocado and blend it thoroughly in the food-processor with the spinach. Add the mashed curd cheese and liquidize again. Then mix in the garlic and lemon juice to taste, and stir in the chopped spring onions. Season to taste with salt and paprika. Chill for a while before serving.

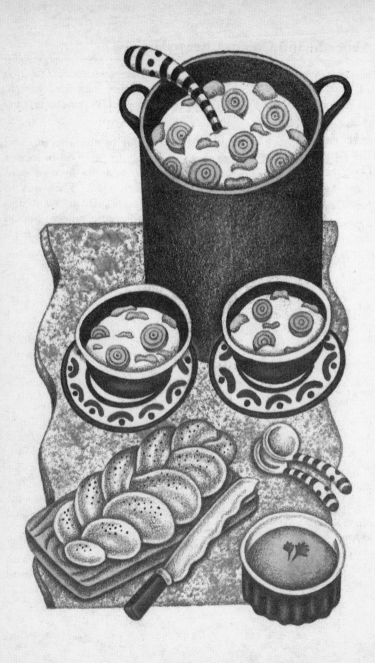

STARTERS AND SOUPS

Mushroom Pâté

Serves 2

1 medium-sized onion,
chopped

2 cloves of garlic, chopped

Butter, 50 g (2 oz)

1 thick slice wholemeal
bread

A little milk

Mushrooms, 100 g (4 oz)

Sea salt, 1 tsp

Mixed herbs, 2 tsp
chopped

A little grated nutmeg and
black pepper

Wholesome and full of flavour, this mushroom pâté also has a mouth-watering softness on the palate. Serve it on granary toast, with a slice of tomato as garnish – or take it on a picnic.

Stew the chopped onion and garlic gently in 25 g (1 oz) of the butter until soft. Meanwhile, soak the bread in a little milk, and chop the mushrooms. Now fry the mushrooms with the onion and garlic, squeeze the bread and crumble it into the pan. Add the chopped herbs, salt, pepper and a little grated nutmeg.

Cook all together for a minute or two, then liquidize the mixture, together with the rest of the butter. Press into a small dish and refrigerate for several hours.

Tomato and Orange Soup

Serves 2–3

1 onion, finely chopped
1 clove of garlic, finely sliced
Vegetable oil, 3 tbs
Canned tomatoes, 400 g (14 oz)
Grated rind of 1 orange
Orange juice, 150 ml (¼ pint)
Vegetable stock, 600 ml (1 pint)
Salt and pepper

This soup is a soft orangey-red colour, and has a wonderfully refreshing flavour. Light, interesting food that will not damage the bank account!

Soften the onions and garlic in the oil over a low heat for 6–8 minutes. Stir in the tomatoes with the juices from the can and the orange rind. Heat through, mixing well, and simmer for 3–4 minutes. Liquidize in the blender with the orange juice, then return to the pan. Heat through, adding the stock as you stir the soup. Season to taste and simmer for 5 minutes before serving.

Nutty Garlic Canapés

Serves 2

Crunchy peanut butter, 2 tbs
Sunflower margarine or butter, 25 g (1 oz) melted
1 clove of garlic, crushed
Dried mixed herbs, 1 tbs
2 thin slices of bread, crusts removed
Vegetable oil for frying
Salt and pepper

Definitely moreish, these nutty delicacies, full of herbs and garlic, make an irresistible snack to go with a drink before a meal.

Put the peanut butter into the blender with the melted margarine or butter, garlic and herbs, and liquidize to a paste. Season to taste.

Cut each slice of bread into small squares and fry gently in vegetable oil until golden on both sides. Drain and dry on kitchen paper.

Heap a little of the nutty garlic mixture on to each square of fried bread and the canapés are ready to serve.

Julia's Pâté

Serves 2

2 eggs, beaten

Butter or sunflower margarine, 15 g (½ oz)

Leeks, 175 g (6 oz) cooked and chopped

½ a canned pimento

Summer herbs, 1 tbs finely chopped

6 black olives, stoned, to garnish

Salt to taste

This very unusual pâté, made with leeks, herbs and pimento, is lovely food. The distinctive flavours of the ingredients are not, however, overpowering – they are well balanced by the eggs, which bind them into a soft consistency.

Scramble the eggs in the butter or margarine until lightly set, then leave to cool on a plate. Liquidize them, with the leeks, pimento and herbs, to a purée. Season to taste. Pack into a small dish, and garnish with the olives. Sensational with granary toast.

Spicy Carrot Soup

Serves 2

Carrots, 350 g (12 oz) cooked

Vegetable stock, 600 ml (1 pint)

Garam masala, 2 tsp

Salt to taste

For all its simplicity – and economy! – this is an exceptional soup. It takes hardly any time to prepare, yet the results are sensational. Lovely with hot granary bread straight from the oven.

Liquidize the carrots with the stock and the garam masala. Heat gently, stirring, for 5 minutes, then season to taste with salt. Simmer for a further 5 minutes before serving.

Leek and Potato Soup

Serves 3–4

Leeks, 350 g (12 oz) cooked

Potatoes, 350 g (12 oz) cooked

Vegetable stock, 1.2 litres (2 pints)

Salt and pepper

A fine, warming soup for cold weather, which is simply prepared and also freezes very well. Served with warm, fresh bread it makes a meal in itself.

Liquidize the vegetables with half of the stock. Heat through in a saucepan, stirring in the rest of the stock. Simmer for 3–4 minutes, then season to taste with salt and pepper.

Flageolet and Garlic Dip

Serves 2–3

Canned flageolets, 175 g (6 oz)

Ground cumin, coriander and turmeric, 2 tsp each

1 large clove of garlic, crushed

Juice of ½ a lemon

Olive oil, 3–4 tbs

Salt

The soft green colour of flageolets is highlighted by turmeric, and the rest of the spicing gives this dip a vaguely oriental feeling. It is rich, nourishing food best served with crudités and bread-sticks or pitta bread.

Put the flageolets, spices, garlic and lemon juice into the blender and whizz to a thick purée with some of the juices from the can. Gradually stir the oil into the mixture to thin out to a dipping consistency. Season to taste.

Tabbouleh

Serves 2

*Bulgar wheat, 100 g
(4 oz) soaked in warm
water for 30 minutes*

1 onion, finely chopped

*1 small bunch of parsley,
finely chopped*

Mint, 1 tbs finely chopped

Olive oil, 2–3 tbs

Lemon juice, 2 tbs

Salt and pepper

*Wedges of tomato, olives
and a sprig of parsley to
garnish*

Middle Eastern cuisine is responsible for this lovely recipe. Serve it as a starter, with warm pitta bread, or as a simple lunch dish with a tomato and onion salad.

Drain the bulgar wheat thoroughly. Mix with the chopped onion and season to taste with salt and pepper. Stir in the chopped herbs and then add the olive oil and lemon juice slowly, stirring thoroughly.

Serve surrounded by wedges of tomato and black olives, and garnish with a sprig of parsley.

Pumpkin Soup

Serves 3–4

*Pumpkin, 450 g (1 lb)
peeled and de-seeded*

*Butter or margarine, 25 g
(1 oz)*

1 onion, thinly sliced

*2 medium tomatoes, peeled
and chopped*

Stock, 1.2 litres (2 pints)

Salt and pepper

When pumpkins are abundant in late autumn, this soup makes cheap, warming and nourishing food. It is a soft golden-yellow colour, rich and satisfying food for chilly weather.

Dice the pumpkin flesh into small cubes. Melt the butter in a large pan, and add the pumpkin and the sliced onion. Stir well. Add the tomatoes and season to taste with salt and pepper. Pour over the stock, cover and simmer gently for 30–40 minutes until the pumpkin is completely soft. Purée in the blender, check the seasoning and it is ready to serve.

Garlicky Mushroom Croûtes

Serves 2

1 small onion, chopped very
finely

Butter, 40 g (1½ oz)

Mushrooms, 175 g (6 oz)
chopped very finely

1 clove of garlic, crushed

Parsley, 2 tbs finely
chopped

Parmesan, 1 tbs grated

2 eggs

Fromage frais, 50 g
(2 oz)

Salt and pepper

2 large crusty rolls

Butter, 25 g (1 oz)
melted

Crisp, golden bread shells enclose a mouth-wateringly smooth, light filling of mushrooms and fromage frais with herbs. This starter is a delight – no problem with leftovers here.

Cook the chopped onion in the butter gently for 4–5 minutes until soft and translucent, then turn the heat up and toss in the chopped mushrooms. Stir-fry so that they are well coated with the butter, and cook for 3–4 minutes until they are crisp and hot. Turn the heat down and stir in the garlic and parsley. Cook for a minute or so gently, then add the Parmesan.

Beat the eggs thoroughly and scramble them lightly into the mushroom mixture so that they are creamy, then cool. Mash the fromage frais and combine with the mushroom mixture. Season to taste and leave to one side.

Cut the rolls in half and scoop out the bread in the middle, leaving the crusts as shells. Brush with melted butter and crisp in a warm oven for 10 minutes. Pile the warm mushroom mixture into them and serve at once.

SNACKS

Sandwich fillings

There is more to a sandwich than just a sandwich.

You can bake sandwiches, toast sandwiches, fry sandwiches, layer sandwiches, make open sandwiches ... Making sandwiches can be a creative activity!

Try some of these fillings to make a change from more traditional ones:

◇ A purée of cottage cheese, mixed with grated Cheddar, chopped spring onions and fresh herbs

◇ Cold scrambled eggs with chopped spring onions or fresh herbs

◇ Chopped hard-boiled eggs in mustardy mayonnaise, with chopped fennel

◇ Thinly sliced smoked cheese and pineapple

◇ Cream cheese and chutney with a little finely chopped dried apricot

◇ Cream cheese and gherkin

◇ Cold scrambled eggs with sweetcorn

◇ Ratatouille

◇ Slices of fresh tomato with feta cheese

◇ Sliced mushrooms, quickly sautéed in butter and left to cool

◇ Shredded lettuce and chopped pineapple in a little mayonnaise

◇ A purée of watercress with soft-boiled egg and a little mayonnaise to mix

◇ Finely chopped watercress with fromage blanc

◇ Finely sliced celery, cream cheese and chopped dried apricots.

For toasted sandwiches

◇ Creamed mushrooms with a little grated Parmesan

◇ Sliced tomatoes with grated cheese

◇ Crunchy peanut butter (you can also bake these: 150°C/300°F/ gas mark 2 for 15 minutes, and they crisp up on the outside and are soft and crunchy inside . . .)

◇ Sliced banana.

Toasts

To ring the changes with hot buttered toast:

◇ Sprinkle a little cinnamon and brown sugar crystals on to hot buttered toast, and pass fleetingly under a grill

◇ Butter slices of bread and bake them at 150°C/300°F/gas 2 for 20–25 minutes until golden and crisp

◇ Top hot buttered toast with slices of tomato and mozzarella, and grill lightly.

Fried sandwiches

◇ Make your sandwich in the normal way, using your chosen filling. Fry it in hot, light vegetable oil until crisp and golden on both sides. Dry on paper towels and eat immediately.

Special picnic loaf

Cut all the crust off a fresh sandwich loaf, white or brown according to taste. Slice it LENGTHWISE into 5 mm ($\frac{1}{4}$ inch) slices. Spread with a little butter or margarine and fill each layer with a chosen salad filling, lightly dressed with mayonnaise. Reconstitute the loaf and wrap it in cling-film. Chill well before eating. To serve it, cut downwards in slices.

Open sandwiches

Make these sandwiches in the Scandinavian style, using crispbread and spreading it with mayonnaise, or with the sunflower butter below. Pile a salad or cheese mixture of your choice on top, and eat as fresh as possible.

Open baguettes

Slice a fresh French stick in half lengthwise, and butter lightly. Cover with a thick layer of mushrooms lightly sautéed in garlic butter with a little parsley, cooled.

Sunflower butter

Using equal quantities of sunflower seeds to butter or margarine, toast the sunflower seeds until they are browned all over. Cool. Melt the butter, and liquidize the two together in the blender to a smooth paste. Pack into a container and chill.

HOT SNACKS

Baked potatoes

These make satisfying and nutritious food for a simple meal. Top them with a pile of grated cheese, or just eat them with butter or margarine. Alternatively you can stuff them with creamed mushrooms or creamed leeks, or baked beans if you are really hungry!

Deep-fried potato skins

Bake the potatoes for $1\frac{1}{4}$ hours at 200°C/400°F/gas 6, and cool a little. Scoop out the potato flesh and use it for the potato hash on p. 25, or for bubble and squeak (p. 25). Cut the skins into small squares of about $1\frac{1}{2}$ inches, and deep-fry in very hot oil until crisp. Drain on paper towels and eat hot as a snack.

You can also eat these cold, using them to dip into the avocado and cream cheese dip (p. 7), or the flageolet and garlic dip (p. 12).

Puff pastry rolls

The vegetarian answer to the sausage roll . . .

For the fillings, use any of the following, mixed with a little curd cheese, and egg yolk to bind:

◇ Sliced mushrooms

◇ Grated cheese

◇ Chopped spring onion and herbs

◇ Canned sweetcorn, drained

◇ Chopped cooked leeks.

Roll puff pastry thinly into rectangles measuring about 5 × 10 cm (2 × 4 inches). Place the filling of your choice in the centre, roll the pastry up around it and seal the edge with water, pressing the seam together with a fork. Brush the top with beaten egg and sprinkle with sesame or poppy seeds. Bake at 200°C/400°F/gas 6 for about 10 minutes, until golden and puffed. Cool on a rack for a few minutes before eating.

Soufflé toasts

Cut sliced bread into rounds with a pastry cutter. Butter on the underside.

Beat one egg white per person stiffly and fold in some finely grated cheese, finely chopped pepper or spring onion, and fresh herbs and seasonings to taste. Heap this mixture on to the unbuttered side of the bread and bake in a very hot oven, 230°C/450°F/gas 8, for 5–8 minutes, until well risen. Eat immediately.

Fried cheese

Cut slices of waxy cheese – Bel Paese gives the best results – about 5 mm ($\frac{1}{4}$ inch) thick. Dip in flour, beaten egg and breadcrumbs, and fry in very hot, light vegetable oil until crisp on the outside and still gooey inside. Drain on kitchen paper and eat immediately.

Cheddar and Edam work quite well, and it is worth experimenting with the Greek cheese halloumi, too.

Welsh rarebit

A simple mixture of beaten eggs (one or two per person, according to appetite), a little milk, grated cheese, and salt and pepper is heaped on to toast and grilled until set. Served with a tossed salad it makes a perfect snack for lunch or supper.

POTATO
DISHES

Grated Potato Patties

Serves 2–3

Potatoes, 450 g (1 lb)
peeled and coarsely grated

2 eggs, lightly beaten

1 small onion, grated

Cornflour, 1 tbs

Salt and pepper

Freshly grated nutmeg,
¼ tsp

Ground-nut oil for frying

These are gorgeous. There is something very special about the taste of grated raw potato lightly cooked, and these patties are distinctly moreish. You probably won't have any leftovers!

Soak the grated potatoes in cold water. Drain them through a large sieve, pressing out all the water, then pat them dry with kitchen paper.

Mix the beaten egg, onion and cornflour together and season with salt, pepper and nutmeg. Stir in the grated potato.

In a small, heavy-bottomed frying-pan heat a little oil until it is hot, then drop the mixture 2–3 tbs at a time into the pan, and flatten each pancake with the back of a spoon. Cook on both sides until golden. Drain on kitchen paper and keep hot in a low oven until ready to eat.

Cheesy Potatoes

Serves 2–3

Potatoes, 350 g (12 oz)
cooked and sliced

Cheddar, 40 g (1½ oz)
grated

Parsley, 1 tbs chopped

Onion, 1 tbs finely chopped

2 eggs

Milk, 300 ml (½ pint)

Granary breadcrumbs,
1 tsp

Salt and pepper

This dish of potatoes, with cheese and onion and parsley, is satisfying and warming food. It makes a simple supper dish whose tastiness belies its economy.

Arrange a layer of the sliced potatoes on the bottom of a small ovenproof dish. Sprinkle with some of the cheese, parsley and onion, and season with salt and pepper. Beat the eggs, and stir the milk into them. Pour a little of this over the potatoes in the dish. Continue with the layers, finishing with a layer of cheese. Sprinkle the breadcrumbs over the top and bake at 180°C/350°F/gas 4 for 30 minutes.

Potatoes under the Grill

Serves 2

4 medium potatoes, peeled

Unsalted butter, 40 g
(1½ oz)

1 clove of fresh garlic

Sea salt and freshly ground
black pepper

A lightly grilled circle of thinly sliced potatoes is simply flavoured with garlic and passed under the grill with a little butter on top. A lovely supper dish served with a tossed salad.

Slice the raw potatoes as thinly as possible and, using a biscuit cutter, cut out circles.

In a heavy pan heat enough butter, about 25 g (1 oz), to cover the bottom. Sauté the potato circles on both sides, one layer at a time, until they are just cooked.

Butter a small ovenproof dish, and rub the bottom with a cut clove of garlic. Melt the remaining butter. Make layers of overlapping potato circles, brushing them with melted butter and seasoning with salt and pepper. Then brush with the melted butter. Place under the grill for about 1 minute or until they are golden brown.

Potato Hash

Serves 2–3

Potatoes, 450 g (1 lb) cooked

Butter or margarine, 50 g (2 oz)

Milk, 100 ml (4 fl. oz)

Salt and pepper

Oil for frying

You can use leftover baked potatoes for this dish if you have them around. The simple device of browning a cake of mashed potatoes until it is golden on both sides is one of the most delicious ways of cooking potatoes. Warming, satisfying food.

Mash the potatoes thoroughly with the butter or margarine, and beat to a smooth purée with the milk. Season well with salt and pepper. Put a little oil into a heavy-bottomed pan and press the mixture down into it. Fry until the bottom is well browned, over a very low heat – about 20 minutes. Turn over and brown the second side for a further 20 minutes or so. Turn out on to a warm serving-dish.

Bubble and Squeak

Serves 2

Large old potatoes, 350 g (12 oz) peeled

Unsalted butter, 40 g (1½ oz) softened

Milk, 150 ml (¼ pint)

Leftover cooked Brussels sprouts or spring-greens, 175 g (6 oz) chopped

Vegetable oil, 1 tbs

Salt, pepper and grated nutmeg

A traditional country recipe, bubble and squeak brings back childhood memories. It has justifiably found its place in English cookery, being tasty and satisfying food – at the lowest possible cost.

Cook the potatoes in salted boiling water for 15–20 minutes until soft and mushy. Drain. Mash the potatoes thoroughly with the butter and milk, and fold in the prepared greens. Season liberally with salt and pepper and grated nutmeg.

Grease a large, heavy-bottomed pan with the oil, heat it gently and then pack the mixture into the pan. Cover with a lid and cook over a gentle heat for 20–30 minutes until the underside is completely browned and crisp. Invert on to a serving-dish and it is ready to eat.

Potatoes Annette with Oeufs sur le Plat

Serves 2

Potatoes, 350 g (12 oz) peeled

Butter, 25 g (1 oz)

2–4 eggs

Salt and pepper

A crispy cake of julienne potatoes cooked in butter makes a delicious base for lightly cooked eggs. A perfect supper dish which costs next to nothing, a memorable meal served with a soft lettuce salad and some fresh bread.

Cut the potatoes into strips ('julienne'). Wash them in cold water and dry thoroughly. Season with salt and pepper. Heat the butter in a heavy frying pan and sauté the potatoes until they are well coated, then press them down into a cake

with the back of a fork. Brown on one side only over a very low heat, covered with a lid, for 30 minutes. When well browned, loosen around the edges and carefully invert on to a platter, and keep warm.

Put a little more butter into the pan and heat gently. Break one or two eggs per person into the pan and cook through gently until they set lightly, without browning the whites (*oeufs sur le plat* are a far cry from a fried egg!). Serve on wedges of the potato cake.

Baby Potato Pancakes

Serves 2–3

Potatoes, 225 g (8 oz) cooked

Sunflower margarine, 25 g (1 oz)

Milk, 3–4 tbs

1 large egg, beaten

Crème fraîche, 2 tbs

Salt and pepper

Melted unsalted butter

These little rounds of golden-brown, puffed potato mixture are very scrumptious and take some resisting! Warming food for cold weather, they are lovely with coleslaw or a tomato and onion salad.

Put the potatoes in the blender with the margarine and the milk and work to a smooth purée. Add the beaten egg and crème fraîche and liquidize again. Season to taste with salt and pepper.

Heat a griddle or a large heavy pan over a moderate heat until it is hot, and brush it with melted butter. Stir the potato batter, drop it in tablespoonfuls on to the griddle to form small rounds, and cook the pancakes until bubbles appear on the surface. Add more melted butter as necessary. Turn the pancakes, and cook them on the other side until they are golden. Transfer them to a platter and keep them warm, covered, in a very low oven until ready to serve.

Galette of Potatoes and Tomatoes

Serves 2–3

*1 medium onion, finely
sliced*

Oil for sautéeing

3 sticks of celery, diced

*Potatoes, 350 g (12 oz)
peeled and sliced 3 mm
(⅛ inch) thick*

*Tomatoes, 225 g (8 oz)
skinned (p. 67) and finely
chopped*

1 clove of garlic, crushed

Dried mixed herbs to taste

Salt and pepper

This recipe has invariably proved to be
very popular – and rightly so. The combination of potato, celery and tomatoes,
highlighted by garlic and herbs, is a memorable one. Serve it either as a meal in
itself, with a salad, or as a side-dish.

Sauté the sliced onion in 2 tbs of the oil
over a gentle heat for 5 minutes until it
begins to brown lightly. Add the celery
and cook for a further 5 minutes. Remove
from the pan.

Fry the sliced potatoes in 3 tbs more
hot oil, adding more as needed, shaking
the pan until they begin to brown. Then
lower the heat, cover with a lid and cook
for 5–10 minutes more until the potatoes
are tender. Season to taste.

Then stir in the tomatoes, garlic and
herbs, along with the onion and celery
mixture, and cook for 5 minutes, stirring
all the time. Put into a heatproof dish and
finish under a hot grill for 3–4 minutes.

Minted Pea and New Potato Salad

Serves 2–3

*Small new potatoes, 350 g
(12 oz) scrubbed*

Wine vinegar, 1 tbs

Olive oil, 2 tbs

*Frozen peas, 175 g (6 oz)
lightly cooked*

Mayonnaise, 5 tbs

*Fresh mint leaves, 2 tbs
finely chopped*

Salt and pepper

A potato salad with a difference, this is a delightful summer dish. New potatoes are mixed with lightly cooked peas and some fresh mint, and lightly dressed with oil and vinegar. Lovely with a tossed salad and warm bread.

Simmer the new potatoes for about 5 minutes, or until tender but still firm and crisp. Drain. While the potatoes are still warm, quarter them and halve the quarters. In a bowl drizzle the warm potatoes with the vinegar and the oil, season them with salt and pepper, and toss them carefully to coat them with the marinade. Let the potatoes marinate, covered and chilled, for at least 2 hours or overnight. Then add the peas, mayonnaise, mint, and salt and pepper to taste and stir the mixture carefully. Transfer the salad to a salad bowl and let it come to room temperature.

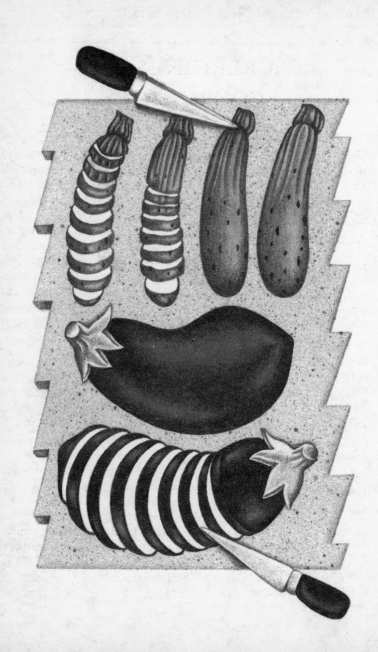

AUBERGINES AND COURGETTES

Aromatic Aubergines

Serves 2–3

For the tomato sauce
1 large onion, sliced very thinly

Olive oil, 2 tbs

Canned tomatoes, 400 g (14 oz) drained and finely chopped

1 bay leaf

Dried thyme, 1 tsp

Orange peel, ½ tsp grated

Pinch of saffron

1 clove of garlic, crushed

Salt

2 good-sized aubergines, quartered and sliced

Olive oil for frying

Gruyère, 75 g (3 oz) sliced very thinly

In this delectable dish, sautéed slices of aubergine are covered with an aromatic tomato sauce and baked with a topping of cheese. It makes a wonderful meal served with a tossed salad and some fresh granary rolls.

Soften the onion in the oil for about 10 minutes, covered, until translucent but not browned. Stir in the tomatoes and add the herbs, orange peel, saffron, garlic and salt. Simmer gently for 30 minutes, then liquidize and leave to stand over a very low heat while you prepare the aubergines.

Sauté the aubergine slices in olive oil until browned on both sides. Drain and dry on kitchen paper.

Arrange the aubergine slices in layers, covering each layer with the tomato sauce and topping with the cheese slices. Cover with foil and bake at 190°C/375°F/ gas 5 for 20 minutes.

Aubergines in Creole Sauce

Serves 2–3

2 medium aubergines, sliced

Sunflower oil for frying

Fried breadcrumbs, 3 tbs

For the creole sauce
Butter or sunflower
margarine, 40 g (1½ oz)

½ a green pepper, de-
seeded and chopped

½ an onion, chopped

1 clove of garlic, crushed

Canned tomatoes, 400 g
(14 oz) finely chopped

1 bay leaf

Pinch each of cloves, salt,
pepper, chilli powder and
sugar

Browned slices of aubergine, sprinkled with breadcrumbs and baked until golden, are served with an exotic, spiced tomato sauce. Lovely with a crisp salad and some noodles or rice.

Fry the aubergine slices in oil until lightly browned on the outside and tender inside. Place in a well-greased baking-dish and cover with the sauce. Sprinkle with the breadcrumbs and bake at 180°C/350°F/gas 4 for 15–20 minutes.

To make the sauce, melt the butter or margarine and cook the pepper, onion and garlic in it for about 5 minutes, stirring, until they begin to soften. Add the tomatoes with the juices from the can and the bay leaf and season with the spices. Heat through and simmer gently for 10 minutes before using.

Golden Aubergines

Serves 2–3

Aubergines, 450 g (1 lb)
sliced

Olive oil for frying

Shallots, 100 g (4 oz)
finely chopped

1 clove of garlic, finely
chopped

2 sprigs of parsley,
chopped

Breadcrumbs, 50 g (2 oz)

Salt and pepper

A simple dish of aubergines, fried until golden, is topped with a mouth-watering mixture of chopped shallots, garlic, parsley and breadcrumbs. Delicious with a tomato and onion salad, some tossed lettuce and warm granary bread.

Fry the sliced aubergines briskly in the olive oil for 2–3 minutes on each side. Cook a few slices at a time. When all the aubergine slices are cooked, return them to the pan.

Mix the shallots, garlic, parsley and breadcrumbs together. Sprinkle this mixture over the aubergines, season and cook over a low heat for a further 10 minutes.

Aubergines en Persillade

Serves 2–3

Aubergines, 450 g (1 lb) peeled

Olive oil for frying

Breadcrumbs, 25 g (1 oz)

Spring onions, 1 tbs chopped

1–2 cloves of garlic, crushed

Fresh thyme or oregano, 1 tbs chopped

Parsley, 2 tbs chopped

Salt

This is a simple, rather classic way of sautéeing aubergines with garlic, parsley, spring onions and breadcrumbs. Its mouth-watering flavours and irresistible textures make a lovely supper dish, served with a tomato salad and hot, soft rolls.

Cut the aubergines into large cubes. Sauté in hot olive oil, shaking the pan frequently until browned all over on the outside and tender inside. Dry on kitchen paper and keep warm. Fry the breadcrumbs in more oil until golden all over, add the spring onions, garlic and herbs and then return the aubergines to the pan. Toss over a moderately high heat until the aubergines are sizzling, add salt to taste, then toss in the parsley and serve in a hot dish.

Aubergine Loaf

Serves 3–4

Aubergine, 350 g (12 oz)

3 eggs

Breadcrumbs, 75 g (3 oz)

Grated cheese, 50 g (2 oz)

Basil, 2 tbs freshly chopped

Olive oil, 100 ml (4 fl. oz)

2 cloves of garlic, crushed

Soy sauce, 1 tbs

Parsley, 2 tbs chopped

Salt and pepper

Most vegetable 'loaves' take an eternity to make, but this one is the exception. Everything goes into the blender, and it is made in next to no time. The result is outstandingly good, a loaf that is delicious hot, warm or cold. You can also make it using mushrooms instead of the aubergines, and the result is also memorable.

Cut the aubergine into pieces and mince in the blender. Put into a bowl. Whizz all the rest of the ingredients in the blender and fold in the minced aubergine. Bake in a greased loaf tin (500 g or 1 lb) at 200°C/400°F/gas 6 for 20 minutes, then at 180°C/350°F/gas 4 for a further 15 minutes or until a knife comes out clean from the centre. Cover with a cloth for 10 minutes, then turn out of the tin.

Aubergines in Sesame Sauce

Serves 2

Sesame seeds, 2 tbs

Soy sauce, 1 tbs

4 small aubergines

Vegetable oil for deep-frying

Sesame seeds to garnish

Browned sesame seeds, pounded with a little soy sauce, make an interesting coating for deep-fried aubergines, and give them an added subtlety of flavour. Serve them warm, with a rice dish – or chilled, with a salad meal.

In a small heavy pan shake the sesame seeds over a moderate heat, stirring and shaking the pan, for 4–5 minutes until golden. Reserve $\frac{1}{4}$ tsp of the sesame seeds and transfer the rest to a mortar. Crush them with the soy sauce.

Cut the aubergines in half lengthwise, and cut each half diagonally into thirds. Deep-fry the aubergine in very hot vegetable oil for 1 minute or until just tender. Dry on paper towels. While the aubergine is still warm toss it with the sesame mixture. Put on to a serving-dish and garnish with the reserved sesame seeds.

Stuffed Courgettes

Serves 2–3

3 medium courgettes

Onion, 75 g (3 oz) chopped

Olive oil, 1½ tbs

Ground almonds, 40 g (1½ oz)

Breadcrumbs, 25 g (1 oz)

Gruyère, 75 g (3 oz) grated

1 large egg, beaten

Parmesan, 15 g (½ oz) grated

Flaked almonds, 15 g (½ oz) browned

Salt, pepper and ground cloves

Courgettes lend themselves to stuffing in many imaginative ways. This particular mixture is nutty and cheesy, a delicate and appetizing filling for blanched courgettes. A lovely summer dish that can be served hot or warm.

Blanch the courgettes in boiling water for 5 minutes, then cut them lengthwise and cool a little. Scoop out the inner flesh carefully with a grapefruit knife and chop it very finely.

Cook the onions gently in the oil until they are soft and sweet, about 10 minutes. Stir in the courgette flesh and cook for another 5 minutes. Add the ground almonds, breadcrumbs and cheese and stir until well mixed together. Mix in the beaten egg so that the mixture is soft but firm.

Fill the courgette halves with the stuffing and sprinkle with Parmesan. Garnish with the browned flaked almonds and bake at 200°C/400°F/gas 6 for 15 minutes.

Courgettes with Tarragon and Cheese

Serves 2–3

Courgettes, 450 g (1 lb) sliced

Butter or sunflower margarine, 40 g (1½ oz)

Shallots, 2 tbs finely chopped

Tarragon, 2 tbs chopped, and a sprig to garnish

Single cream, 150 ml (¼ pint)

Parmesan or Cheddar, 25 g (1 oz) grated

Salt and pepper

There is a delicacy and refinement about this dish, which is based on a classic French recipe. Shallots, tarragon and a little cream, and a topping of grated cheese, make a wonderful combination with sliced courgettes.

Sauté the courgettes in the butter or sunflower margarine until lightly browned and tender, and season with a little salt and pepper. Sprinkle on the shallots and tarragon and pour in the cream. Heat through for 5–6 minutes, then pour into a serving-dish. Sprinkle the grated cheese over the top and brown quickly under a hot grill. Serve garnished with a sprig of tarragon.

Golden Courgettes with Cheese

Serves 2–3

1 medium onion, chopped

Oil, 2 tbs

Pinch of saffron

Yellow courgettes, 450 g (1 lb) sliced

Cheddar, 100 g (4 oz) grated

2 eggs, beaten

Salt and pepper

The golden colour of this dish is as appetizing as its flavours – saffron adding its gold to the yellowness of the courgettes. The dish is delectable with new potatoes and a leafy side-salad.

Soften the onion in the oil over a very gentle heat, covered, for about 10 minutes, stirring from time to time. Add the saffron and season to taste with salt and pepper. Steam the courgette slices until tender. Mix the two together and place in a baking-dish. Add the cheese to the beaten eggs and season with salt and pepper. Pour over the vegetables and bake at 190°C/375°F/gas 5 for 20 minutes, until the topping is risen and set.

Courgettes Provençale

Serves 2

Courgettes, 450 g (1 lb)
coarsely grated

Olive oil for frying

2 cloves of garlic, crushed

Parsley, 4 tbs chopped

Croûtons, 3 tbs

Salt and pepper

Croûtons
Thin slices of day-old
bread

Vegetable oil for frying

Grated courgettes make a delicious dish tossed in olive oil with garlic and parsley. Topped with crunchy croûtons, all this needs to complement it is some fresh bread and a crisp side-salad.

Toss the grated courgettes in the olive oil until just tender and very lightly browned. Add the garlic and parsley and heat through. Season with salt and pepper. Cook for a further 1–2 minutes and serve at once, sprinkled with croûtons.

To make the croûtons, cut the crusts off the bread and cut the slices into tiny cubes. Heat the oil in a frying-pan – put in a generous amount since the bread soaks it up liberally! Toss the bread dice in the oil, turning until they are golden all over, and crisp. Remove from the pan with a slotted spoon, and dry on paper towels.

For garlic croûtons add a little crushed garlic to the oil before frying.

For special occasions, try cutting the bread into different shapes: heart-shaped or tiny triangles, for example.

MUSHROOM MEDLEY

Simple Mushroom Curry

Serves 2

Oil, 3 tbs

Curry paste, 1 tsp

1 medium onion, chopped

Small button mushrooms, 225 g (8 oz) halved

Frozen peas, 175 g (6 oz) defrosted

Natural yogurt, 125 g (4 oz)

1 small bunch fresh coriander, chopped

Salt to taste

The simple stir-frying of mushrooms and peas with curry paste and yogurt makes an incredibly good dish, garnished with that typically Indian herb, coriander. Serve with basmati rice and some poppadams and it is a feast.

Heat the oil in a heavy pan and stir in the curry paste and the onion. Fry gently until soft. Add the mushrooms, turn the heat up a little and stir-fry for 2 minutes. Add the peas and mix well. Add salt to taste and a little water. Gradually stir in the yogurt and mix well. Simmer over a gentle heat until the sauce thickens and the mushrooms and peas are well cooked. Stir in the chopped coriander and it is ready to serve.

Mushrooms Stroganoff

Serves 2

1 onion, finely chopped

1 clove of garlic, crushed

Butter or sunflower margarine, 25 g (1 oz)

Small button mushrooms, 225 g (8 oz) finely sliced

Moutarde de Meaux, 1–2 tsp

Thick set yogurt, 100 g (4 oz)

Salt

Based on a classic Stroganoff recipe, this version loses the wine (and of course the beef!), and makes a delightful dish with mushrooms, garlic, grainy mustard and thick yogurt. Serve it warm, on a bed of rice, with a side-salad.

Soften the onions and garlic in the butter or sunflower margarine until translucent – about 10 minutes. Add the mushrooms and stir until they are beginning to cook through but are not too soft. Strain off most of the juices, reserving 2 tbs. Stir in the mustard and salt to taste and mix thoroughly. Mix the reserved cooking-juices into the yogurt, and stir into the mushrooms. Heat through and serve warm.

Mushrooms 'Monte Carlo'

Serves 2

Button mushrooms, 225 g (8 oz) washed

Olive oil, 3 tbs

1 small sprig mint, finely chopped

Juice of 1 lemon

Parsley, 3 tbs chopped

Salt and pepper

A light, refreshing supper dish that goes beautifully with eggs or on a bed of rice. Lovely for summer weather, when the cool minty and lemony flavours come into their own. Delicious hot or cold.

Leave the mushrooms whole if small, otherwise halve or quarter them according to size. Heat the oil in a heavy pan, add the mushrooms and cook gently. After 5 minutes, season with salt and pepper and add the chopped mint and lemon juice. Cook until the liquid is reduced. Sprinkle with parsley and serve at once with a plain omelette, scrambled eggs or rice.

Mushroom and Celeriac Salad

Serves 2

Button mushrooms, 175 g
(6 oz)

Juice of half a lemon

Celeriac, 100 g (4 oz)

Various lettuce leaves and
watercress, washed

1 clove of garlic, crushed

Thick Greek yogurt, 2 tbs

Dijon or mild mustard,
1 tbs

Summer herbs, 1 tbs finely
chopped

Salt and pepper to taste

When celeriac is unobtainable, you can use
finely sliced celery heart for this delicious
salad. The mixture is flavoured with garlic,
mild mustard and summer herbs, and is
lovely served with warm granary bread.

Slice or quarter the mushrooms and
sprinkle lemon juice over them. Peel the
celeriac and cut into matchstick-sized pieces
or shred in the food-processor. Drop immediately into water to which you have
added a squeeze of lemon or spoonful of
vinegar to stop it discolouring while you
quickly prepare the rest of the salad.

Arrange the salad leaves on two plates.
Add the crushed garlic to the yogurt. Stir
in the mustard, salt and pepper. Drain the
celeriac and stir into the dressing. Add the
mushrooms and the chopped herbs and
mix well. Pile the mixture on to the salad
leaves and serve as soon as possible.

Spicy Mushroom Salad

Serves 2

Crunchy peanut butter,
1 tbs

Soy sauce, 1 tbs

Raspberry vinegar (see
p. 121), 1 tbs

Dark sesame oil, 3 tbs

Mayonnaise, 2 tbs

Button mushrooms, 225 g
(8 oz) finely sliced

Chopped coriander to
garnish

This salad, made with finely sliced raw
mushrooms, has a highly unusual dressing
based on an Indonesian recipe, with a
touch of originality – some raspberry vinegar. Pile the dressed mushrooms into
soft lettuce leaves, and serve with garlic
bread.

Mix the peanut butter with the soy
sauce, raspberry vinegar and sesame oil
and blend well. Stir into the mayonnaise.
Dress the sliced mushrooms with the mixture, tossing so that they are thoroughly
coated. Leave to stand for at least 2 hours.
Garnish with chopped coriander leaves.

Mushroom Casserole with Wild Rice

Serves 2–3

Wild rice, 175 g (6 oz) washed

Large mushrooms, 350 g (12 oz) sliced

Butter, 75 g (3 oz)

Tomatoes, 175 g (6 oz) skinned (see p. 67) and chopped

Single cream, 5 tbs

Soured cream or yogurt, 5 tbs

Salt, pepper and lemon juice

This delectable casserole of mushrooms, tomatoes and soured cream is served inside a ring of wild rice. The creamy sauce is mopped up by the rice and makes a memorable supper dish.

Drain the washed rice, cover with boiling water in a large saucepan and bring to the boil. Simmer for 5 minutes and leave to stand in the same water for half an hour. Then drain and cover with fresh water, and simmer for about 10–15 minutes until the rice is tender but still crunchy. Drain, and arrange around the edge of a warmed serving-dish. Cover with foil and keep warm while you prepare the mushrooms.

Cut the mushroom slices into strips and toss in the butter over a gentle heat for 6–8 minutes until cooked through but not too soft. Add the single cream and the tomatoes, mix well and simmer together for a further 4–5 minutes. Stir in the soured cream or yogurt and heat through gently. Season to taste with salt, pepper and a little lemon juice.

Place the mushroom mixture in the centre of the serving-dish, surrounded by the wild rice, and it is ready to serve.

Mushrooms with Eggs

Per person

Mushrooms, 150 g (5 oz)
Tarragon vinegar, 1 tbs
2 eggs
Salt and pepper

Mushrooms taste deliciously fresh cooked in this way – steamed in a pan with a little tarragon vinegar, refreshingly sharp. The blandness of the egg is a perfect match for them. This simple supper dish is very quick and easy, yet distinctly different.

Trim the mushrooms, removing the ends of the stalks. Wash them and pat dry. Cut each mushroom into fine slices and put them into a well-greased frying-pan. Sprinkle with the vinegar and season with salt and pepper. Cover, and cook over a gentle heat for about 10 minutes, shaking the pan from time to time.

Drop two eggs into the pan before all the water produced by the mushrooms has evaporated. Leave to cook, uncovered, for a further 3–5 minutes, depending on individual taste.

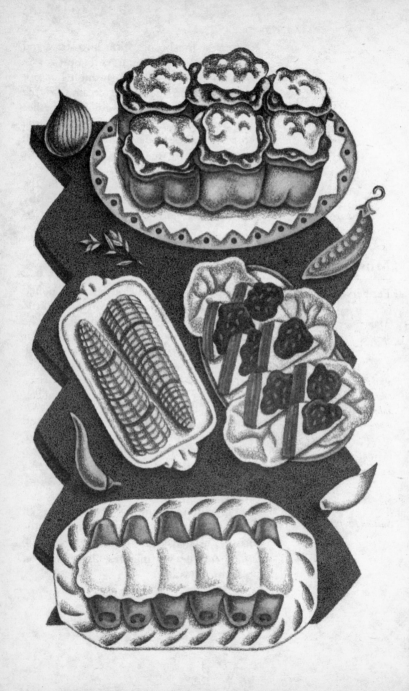

VEGETABLE MAIN COURSES

Melting Vegetable Kebabs

Serves 2–3

*Mixed vegetables, e.g.
mushrooms, courgettes,
tomatoes, celery, shallots,
aubergine, cauliflower,
mange-tout, etc., 750 g
(1½ lb)*

Olive oil, 2–3 tbs

Dried mixed herbs, 1 tbs

*Mozzarella, 75 g (3 oz)
sliced*

Salt and pepper

Crunchy vegetable kebabs make an eye-catching main course, and the final coating of melting mozzarella is quite mouth-watering. Serve them on a bed of rice, with a sauce of your choice (see 'Sauces and Dressings', p. 119).

Slice all the vegetables to bite size and skewer them alternately on to kebab sticks. Brush liberally with olive oil and sprinkle with dried mixed herbs, salt and pepper. Grill under a moderate heat for 10–12 minutes, turning, until the vegetables are cooked through but still slightly crisp. Then finally cover them with slices of mozzarella and brown under the grill. Serve at once.

Vegetables alla Casalinga

Serves 2

Vegetables of your choice, e.g. broccoli, cauliflower, asparagus, French beans, mange-tout, etc., 600 g (1¼ lb)

Butter, 25 g (1 oz) melted

Parmesan, 15 g (½ oz) grated

2 eggs, lightly poached

8 heart-shaped croûtons (see p. 37)

Salt and pepper

A delightful plate of lightly cooked vegetables browned with a little cheese, this simple supper dish is topped with a poached egg and some croûtons. Serve it with a crisp side-salad with a dressing of your choice (see 'Sauces and Dressings', p. 119).

Steam the vegetables of your choice until they are tender. Place them in a warm heatproof dish, pour the melted butter over and sprinkle with the Parmesan. Season with salt and pepper and brown quickly under a medium grill. Serve each portion with a poached egg and four heart-shaped croûtons.

Chilean Sweetcorn Parcels

Serves 3–4

8 large Chinese leaves

Canned sweetcorn, 400 g (14 oz) drained

Milk 4–5 tbs

2 eggs, beaten

Fresh herbs (e.g. marjoram, basil, coriander, etc.), 2 tbs finely chopped

Pepper to taste

This recipe was given to me by a friend who lived in Chile for several years, and it has become a firm favourite. A sweetcorn paste tasting of fresh herbs is poached inside a wrapping of Chinese leaves. A delicious supper dish. Serve on rice or with noodles.

Steam the Chinese leaves for a minute or two until supple but not too soft. Liquidize all the rest of the ingredients together to a paste. Divide the mixture into eight and put spoonfuls into the centre of each leaf. Wrap up like a spring-roll, with the ends folded in, and secure with a wooden cocktail stick. Steam over hot water for 20–25 minutes until the filling is set.

Broccoli Niçoise

Serves 2

Broccoli, 450 g (1 lb) cut into spears

Onions, 100 g (4 oz) very finely chopped

Olive oil, 2 tbs

1 clove of garlic, crushed

2 large triangles of puff pastry, cooked

Breadcrumbs, 40 g (1½ oz) fried until golden in sunflower oil

Salt and pepper

This classic French way of cooking vegetables, with onion, garlic and fried breadcrumbs, is quite delectable piled on to triangles of puff pastry and served piping hot.

Steam the broccoli until tender, about 5 minutes. Soften the onions in the oil over a very gentle heat, covered, stirring from time to time until they are soft and sweaty. This will take about 10 minutes. Stir in the garlic and season with a little salt and pepper. Toss in the cooked broccoli spears and place in a warm dish on the triangles of puff pastry. Serve sprinkled with the fried breadcrumbs.

Golden Stuffed Peppers

Serves 2

2 yellow peppers

Courgettes, 175 g (6 oz) grated

1 small onion, chopped

Canned sweetcorn, 225 g (8 oz) drained and puréed

Cheddar, 50 g (2 oz) finely grated

1 egg, beaten

Pepper

Yellow peppers have a gentler, sweeter flavour than red or green, and this mellowness is taken up by the grated courgettes and sweetcorn in the stuffing. The stuffed peppers are covered with grated cheese and baked – a delicious meal that you can serve with rice or potatoes and a tossed salad.

Blanch the peppers in boiling water for 5 minutes, then drain, cut in half and de-seed them. Mix the grated courgette and chopped onion into the sweetcorn purée and add half the cheese. Mix well and then stir in the beaten egg. Mix thoroughly and season to taste. Pile into the halved peppers. Sprinkle with the rest of the cheese and bake at 180°C/350°F/gas 4 for 25 minutes. Serve hot.

Spiced Corn on the Cob

Serves 2

For the spice paste
Turmeric, ½ tsp

5-spice, ½ tsp

Pinch of chilli powder

Garam masala, ½ tsp

Ground coriander, 1 tsp

Water, 3 tbs

2 large, tender corn cobs,
cut into 4 pieces

Vegetable oil, 3 tbs

1 small onion, finely
chopped

Fresh root ginger, 1 cm
(½ inch) grated

1 clove of garlic, crushed

Thick set yogurt, 100 g
(4 oz)

Salt

This wonderful recipe is inspired by an idea given to me by an Indian friend. The slices of corn cob are poached in an aromatic, spicy sauce with a yogurt base, and are sumptuously delicious. It makes a complete meal if served with the simple mushroom curry on p. 39.

Mix the spices together and stir into a paste with the water. Fry the corn cob pieces in the oil until browned all over, and set aside. Then fry the onion, ginger and garlic for a few minutes until softened, and stir in the spice paste. Cook gently for 2–3 minutes and then stir in the yogurt gradually. Season to taste with salt and return the corn to the pan. Heat through gently and it is ready to serve.

Broccoli Polish-style

Serves 2

Broccoli spears, 450 g
(1 lb) steamed 'al dente'

1 hard-boiled egg, peeled

Breadcrumbs, 25 g (1 oz)
fried in sunflower oil until
golden

Salt and pepper

The simple device of topping cooked broccoli with chopped hard-boiled egg and fried breadcrumbs makes a light, appetizing meal served with buttered rice and either a side vegetable dish or a tossed salad.

Lay the broccoli spears in a warm dish and season them with salt and pepper. Sieve the egg yolk and chop the white finely. Mix with the hot breadcrumbs and strew over the warm broccoli. Heat through for 5 minutes at 180°C/350°F/gas 4 and serve warm.

Carrots with Soft Cheese

Serves 2–3

Carrots, 450 g (1 lb)

1 bouquet garni

Low-fat fromage blanc,
100 g (4 oz)

Juice of 1 small orange

Black pepper

Grated nutmeg

Small bunch of fresh chives

The really fresh flavours and soft textures of this unusual carrot dish make a lovely meal. Serve it on a bed of noodles, with a side-salad and some fresh bread to mop up the juices.

Peel, wash and cut carrots into strips. Cook in boiling water with the bouquet garni for 3–4 minutes until tender but still crisp. Remove the bouquet garni. Cool while you prepare the sauce.

Season the fromage blanc with the orange juice, pepper, grated nutmeg and chopped chives. Spoon the cold sauce over the warm carrots and serve.

Indonesian Spiced Vegetables

Serves 2–3

For the paste
½ a fresh chilli, seeds removed

Ground coriander, 1 tsp

Flaked almonds, 25 g (1 oz)

Fresh root ginger, 1 cm (½ inch) grated

A small onion, chopped

Thick coconut milk (see p. 54), 300 ml (½ pint)

Chinese cabbage, okra and French beans, 175 g (6 oz) each

Oil, 3 tbs

1 hard-boiled egg to garnish

A stir-fry of summer vegetables is cooked with ginger and spices and coconut milk, making a dish evocative of Indonesian cuisine. Serve it with rice or noodles.

In the blender, grind the spices, herbs, almonds and onion into a paste. Fry the ground paste in the oil for 3–4 minutes, stirring well, then stir in half of the coconut milk. Add the vegetables and stir over a gentle heat for 10 minutes. Then add the rest of the coconut milk and simmer for a further 8–10 minutes. Check the seasoning and serve hot, garnished with chopped hard-boiled egg.

Fennel with Cheese

Serves 2

1 large round fennel bulb

Butter, 15 g (½ oz)

2 shallots, peeled and finely chopped

Milk, 4–5 tbs

Gorgonzola or Dolcelatte cheese, 25 g (1 oz)

Fontina or Caciotta cheese, 25 g (1 oz)

Ricotta cheese, 25 g (1 oz)

A delightful way to eat fennel, where the outer leaves are scoops for an unctuous cheesy filling. This is an unusual, rich dish that requires merely a green salad and some warm bread to go with it.

Cut the fennel in half down the middle. Cook in boiling water for 10 minutes or until tender. Drain. Remove the leaves in the centre, taking great care not to break them. Leave one complete layer of leaves so that a small bowl is formed in which to pour the cheese. The leaves you have removed will serve as scoops to eat the cheese. Some of the broader ones can be cut in half down the middle. Put these to one side.

In a small saucepan melt the butter, and gently fry the shallots until soft. Pour on a little of the milk. Crumble in the blue cheese, cut the Fontina or Caciotta into small cubes, and put these in the pan together with the Ricotta. Stir together, heating gently until melted, adding more milk if required, to make a homogeneous, creamy consistency. Pour into the fennel 'bowls', and finish under a hot grill so that the cheese just begins to brown and bubble.

Crêpes alla Parmigiana Parizzi

Serves 4

Spinach, 100 g (4 oz) trimmed and washed well

Ricotta cheese, 175 g (6 oz)

Parmesan, 4 tbs freshly grated

2 eggs, lightly beaten

8 crêpes (p. 124)

Italian Fontina cheese, 100 g (4 oz) cut into 8 strips

Salt, pepper and grated nutmeg to taste

It's worth while making this dish for friends on a special occasion – it takes a little time to prepare, but every mouthful justifies the effort!

Cook the spinach in its own water for 2–3 minutes, until the leaves are soft. Drain, squeeze dry and chop it. In a bowl combine it well with the Ricotta, 2 tbs of the Parmesan, the eggs, and the nutmeg, salt and pepper to taste.

Spread about 3 tbs of the mixture on each crêpe, put a strip of the Fontina across the centre, and roll up the crêpes to enclose the filling. Arrange them seam side down in one layer in a buttered gratin dish. Sprinkle the remaining Parmesan over the crêpes and bake in the middle of a preheated oven at 220°C/425°F/gas 7 for 15–20 minutes, or until they are puffed and golden.

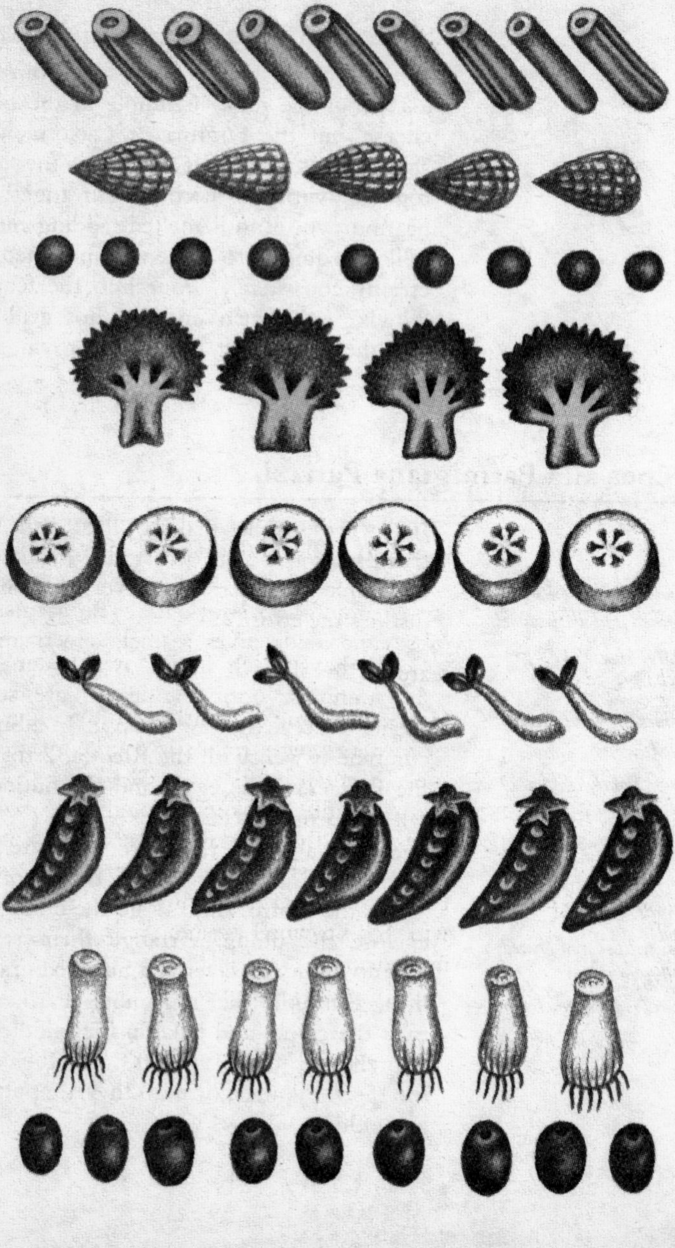

SIDE-VEGETABLES

Mange-tout 'Ali Baba'

Serves 2

Sesame oil, 1–2 tbs

Root ginger, 1 cm
(½ inch) grated

2 spring onions, finely
sliced

Mange-tout, 225 g (8 oz)
topped and tailed

Baby French beans, 100 g
(4 oz)

Fennel, 50 g (2 oz)
chopped

Soy sauce, 1 tbs

White-wine vinegar, 1 tsp

Sesame seeds, 2 tbs toasted

A mouth-watering stir-fry of mange-tout, French beans and fennel with ginger, spring onion and soy sauce. The garnish of sesame seeds gives a final, appetizing texture.

Heat the sesame oil gently with the ginger and spring onion, then stir-fry the mange-tout, French beans and fennel for 5–8 minutes until cooked through but still crisp. Add the soy sauce and white-wine vinegar and stir for a further 2 minutes. Put into a warm serving-dish, sprinkle with the browned sesame seeds and serve immediately.

Cucumber with Coconut

Serves 3

Creamed coconut, 100 g (4 oz)

Hot water, 150 ml (¼ pint)

Turmeric, ½ tsp

½ a dried chilli, soaked in warm water

Cumin seeds, ½ tsp

1 clove of garlic, crushed

Oil, 2 tbs

1 large cucumber, diced

The spiciness of chilli, the flavours of garlic and cumin, are the oriental tastes for this rich and creamy way of cooking cucumber.

Dissolve the creamed coconut in a jug of hot water, and stir in the turmeric. Fry the chilli, cumin seeds and crushed garlic in the oil for 2–3 minutes, then toss the prepared cucumber into the pan. Stir-fry for a minute or so. Pour the coconut milk in and heat through. Simmer for 5 minutes and it is ready to serve.

Piselli alla Toscana

Serves 2

Frozen peas, 225 g (8 oz)

1 clove of garlic, finely chopped

Olive oil, 2 tbs

2 slices of bread, crusts removed

Vegetable oil for frying

Salt and pepper

Lightly cooked peas are tossed in olive oil and garlic, and then mixed with tiny cubes of fried bread. Delicious.

Pour boiling water over the peas and allow to stand for 5 minutes. Drain. Put them into a pan and cook them with the garlic in the olive oil over a gentle heat for 3 minutes. Add a little water and turn the heat up for another minute or two, then season with salt and pepper.

Cut the bread into tiny dice and fry in vegetable oil until golden all over. Drain, and dry on kitchen paper. Toss these croûtons into the peas and serve immediately.

Mange-tout with Fennel

Serves 2

Mange-tout, 225 g (8 oz) topped and tailed

½ a small head of fennel, finely sliced

Sesame oil, 3 tbs

Root ginger, 1 cm (½ inch) finely grated

Soy sauce, 2 tbs

Sesame seeds, 2 tbs toasted under the grill

Summer tastes: delicate mange-tout, distinctive fennel, both stir-fried with ginger and soy sauce. The dish is finished with a sprinkling of sesame seeds.

Slice the mange-tout diagonally and stir-fry with the fennel in the sesame oil until they began to soften. Then stir in the grated ginger and the soy sauce and stir-fry for 2–3 minutes longer. Serve at once, sprinkled with toasted sesame seeds.

Mange-tout with Pine Nuts

Serves 2

Mange-tout, 225 g (8 oz)
topped and tailed

Olive oil, 2 tbs

Pine nuts, 25 g (1 oz)
browned under the grill

Sea salt

A simple stir-fry of mange-tout with browned pine nuts combines two lovely flavours and mouth-wateringly crunchy textures.

Stir-fry the mange-tout in the hot oil for 3–4 minutes until tender but still slightly crisp. Add the browned pine nuts, stir together, and season with a little sea salt. Serve immediately.

Sweet and Sour Chinese Cabbage

Serves 2

Chinese cabbage, 225 g
(8 oz) shredded

½ a fresh chilli, sliced
very finely

Root ginger, 1 cm
(½ inch) peeled and
grated

Ground-nut oil and dark
sesame oil, 2 tbs each

Sugar, 2 tbs

Vinegar, 2 tbs

Salt

Shredded Chinese cabbage is best stir-fried in the wok. It is delightful spiced with chilli and ginger, and goes well with pasta dishes.

Mix the shredded cabbage with the chilli and ginger. Stir-fry in the ground-nut oil for 3 minutes, then add the dark sesame oil, sugar and vinegar. Heat through, stirring, and cook for 2 minutes. Season to taste with salt and serve as soon as possible.

Sautéed Carrots and Celery

Serves 6

Carrots, 350 g (12 oz)
peeled

½ a head of celery,
washed

Olive oil, 2 tbs

1 small onion, thinly sliced

1 bouquet garni

Green olives, 50 g (2 oz)
stoned

Salt and pepper

A delightful, soft mixture of carrots, celery, onions and olives, which makes an excellent side-dish to go with the aubergine loaf on p. 34.

Slice the carrots thinly. Cut the celery sticks into chunks, discarding any stringy pieces.

Heat the oil in a saucepan, add the onion and celery, and cook gently until the onion is golden. Add the carrots, celery and bouquet garni and season to taste. Cover with a lid and cook gently for 10 minutes, shaking the pan frequently.

Add the olives, stir and replace the lid. Simmer very gently for a further 10 minutes.

Leeks with Olives and Parsley

Serves 2

Leeks, 225 g (8 oz)
washed and finely sliced

Olive oil, 3–4 tbs

Vegetable stock, 5 tbs

8–10 black olives, stoned
and sliced

Medium bunch of parsley,
finely chopped

Salt and pepper

Strong flavours here – leeks sautéed with olives and parsley – that are reminiscent of French regional cookery. Lovely with a rice dish, or with the crêpes alla parmigiana parizzi on p. 51.

Sauté the sliced leeks gently in the olive oil, stirring, until they begin to soften, about 6–8 minutes. Stir in the stock and bring to the boil. Simmer gently, uncovered, for 5 minutes. Add the olives and the chopped parsley, and cook, stirring occasionally, for a further 3–4 minutes. Season to taste with salt and pepper and it is ready to serve.

Glazed Carrots with Herbs

Serves 2

Carrots, 225 g (8 oz) trimmed and sliced on the diagonal 0.5 cm (¼ inch) thick

Unsalted butter, 25 g (1 oz)

Vegetable stock, 150 ml (¼ pint)

Sugar, ½ tsp

Fresh parsley, 1 tsp finely chopped

Fresh dill, 1 tsp finely chopped

Salt and pepper

A classic way of cooking carrots, particulary good in summer using fresh baby carrots and parsley from the garden.

Cook the carrots in boiling salted water for 5 minutes, or until they are just tender. Drain them in a colander, and refresh them under running cold water. In a frying-pan toss the carrots in the butter over moderate heat until they are well coated. Add the stock, sugar, and salt and pepper to taste, and cook the mixture over a moderately high heat, tossing the carrots, until the liquid is reduced to a glaze. Stir in the parsley and the dill. Serve hot.

Sesame Green Beans and Peas

Serves 2–3

Unsalted butter, 2 tbs

Vegetable oil, 2 tbs

Frozen peas, 225 g (8 oz) thawed and drained

Green beans, 225 g (8 oz) trimmed and cut crosswise into 0.5 cm (¼ inch) pieces

Sugar, 1 tsp

Sesame seeds, 3 tbs toasted

Dark sesame oil, 1 tbs

Salt and pepper

A delightful combination, with the crunch of browned sesame seeds and the distinctive flavour of dark sesame oil.

Heat the butter with the oil in a pan. Sauté the peas and the beans in the mixture over a moderately high heat, stirring, for 1 minute, until they are coated. Add sugar and heat through gently for a further 4–5 minutes, tossing occasionally. Remove the pan from the heat, stir in the toasted sesame seeds, the sesame oil, and salt and pepper to taste, and transfer the mixture to a heated serving-dish.

Cauliflower al-Shami

Serves 2

½ a large cauliflower
Olive oil, 3–4 tbs
1–2 cloves of garlic, sliced
1 small bunch of coriander, chopped

A superb way of cooking cauliflower, given to me by a Lebanese chef. The florets are stir-fried with olive oil, garlic and lots of fresh coriander, and the result is irresistible.

Cut the cauliflower into tiny florets. Heat the olive oil gently and sauté the sliced garlic in it until soft, about 2–3 minutes. Turn the heat up and stir-fry the cauliflower florets for a further 2–3 minutes, tossing so that they are well coated with the oil. Turn the heat down, partially cover with a lid, and cook until soft, about 4 minutes. Stir in the chopped coriander, toss for 1 minute more, and serve.

STIR-FRYING VEGETABLES, AND A GUIDE TO THE WOK

Stir-frying vegetables – tossing them quickly in a very little hot oil – brings the best out in them. This technique of cooking vegetables retains their texture, their colour and above all their flavour. The process takes a matter of only minutes – the time-consuming part is the preparation, slicing, dicing or shredding them to the desired size. This must all be done just in advance so that the vegetables are ready to hand, since the cooking process is so swift.

To cut or chop the vegetables, the best tools to use are good-quality, very sharp kitchen knives. These are a good investment: cheap knives will not give you the precision and clean cutting-edge that you require. For certain vegetables you can use the julienne blade of a food-processor, although this does tend to cut them very small. A hand-operated julienne-cutter yields better results. The thinner the slices, cubes or shreds, the less the cooking time.

For the best effect, cut the vegetables diagonally, across the grain, and always use vegetables that are perfectly fresh. Courgettes, French beans, cauliflower, broccoli, spring onions, Chinese leaf, cabbage, baby sweetcorn, okra, beansprouts, thinly sliced Brussels sprouts, and mushrooms of all varieties are among the vegetables that lend themselves best to stir-frying.

A dish of stir-fried vegetables, spiced with ginger, garlic or black-bean sauce – or a combination of these – makes a delicious meal in its own right, served with rice or noodles: fresh, healthy, balanced food.

Using a wok is by far the best way to stir-fry vegetables. Its large bowl-shape ensures the even and intense heat that is necessary for successful results. A wok is used 'seasoned' – that is, rather than washing it clean, it is to be wiped with a damp cloth or paper towels, then rubbed with oil all over its surface. At this point heat it gently, and keep rubbing it clean with kitchen paper, adding more oil as needed, until the paper comes off clean. Finish by rubbing a layer of clean oil sparingly into the warm pan. Then set it to one side for the next time that you use it.

To stir-fry vegetables, put a little oil into the wok and distribute it evenly over the surface with the back of a wooden spoon or spatula. Oriental cooks often use ground-nut oil (which is tasteless) for stir-frying, adding the more tasty sesame oil towards the end of the cooking so that it retains all its flavour. The oil should become very hot, almost smoking, before the prepared vegetables are added. Toss them all over the surface of the wok so that they sizzle, moving them from the centre to the sides.

If you are cooking spring onions, ginger and garlic first, to flavour the dish, do not allow the oil to get so hot, otherwise it will burn them.

If your vegetables require light steaming in order to finally cook them through, turn the heat down low, and cover the wok with a lid. Leave for a minute or two for the vegetables to finish cooking.

Always serve stir-fried vegetables as soon as possible, since they do not improve on keeping and are at their best crisp and hot from the pan.

EGGS GALORE

Indonesian Soufflé Omelette

Serves 2–3

Root ginger, peeled and grated 1 cm (½ inch)

1 clove of garlic, crushed

Sesame oil

Chinese cabbage, 75 g (3 oz) shredded

Small button mushrooms, 75 g (3 oz) sliced

Sweetcorn, 50 g (2 oz)

Mange-tout, 50 g (2 oz)

1 fresh chilli, de-seeded and chopped

Dry-roasted peanuts, 40 g (1½ oz) ground

Thin coconut milk (see p. 54), 150 ml (¼ pint)

3 eggs, separated

Salt

Fresh coriander leaves to garnish

Soufflé omelettes are spectacular dishes, yet they are disarmingly simple to prepare. The Indonesian spicing of this dish, and the coconut milk which is so typical of that cuisine, make this a meal to remember. Serve it with a couple of salads of your choice (see 'Composite Salads', on p. 95).

Soften the ginger and garlic in the oil for 2–3 minutes, then toss in the prepared vegetables. Stir until heated through and well coated with the oil, then add the ground peanuts. Stir well. Pour in the coconut milk and simmer for 5 minutes. Remove from the heat, then mix in the beaten egg yolks and stir thoroughly. Season to taste. Fold in the stiffly beaten whites and pour the mixture into a large, well-oiled, heavy frying-pan. Cook over a very gentle heat for 8–10 minutes until puffed and beginning to set. Brown under a hot grill for a minute or two to finish the cooking, and serve immediately garnished with fresh coriander leaves. Cut into wedges for each serving.

Tomato Croûton Omelette

Serves 2

4 eggs

Milk, 3 tbs

2 tomatoes, skinned (see p. 67) and sliced

A few chopped chives

Croûtons, 3 tbs (see p. 37)

Salt and pepper

A little Parmesan to garnish

Blissful summer food. Use tomatoes that are as fresh as possible for the best results here. The crunch of croûtons in the filling is utterly mouth-watering, and gives this omelette a distinction quite its own.

Beat the eggs with the milk and season with salt and pepper. Lightly grease a heavy frying-pan and pour in the mixture. (If you do not have a pan large enough, make two omelettes separately.) As it begins to set, place the sliced tomatoes on top and sprinkle with the chives. Season with salt and pepper and finally toss in the croûtons. Fold the omelette in half and serve as soon as possible, sprinkled with a little grated Parmesan.

Oeufs Mollets with Green Sauce

Serves 2

2 eggs, boiled for 4 minutes

Peas, 75 g (3 oz) cooked

Asparagus, 75 g (3 oz) cooked

Sunflower margarine, 25 g (1 oz) melted

Béchamel sauce (see p. 119), 5 tbs

A little single cream

Salt and pepper

Parsley sprigs to garnish

A sauce of puréed peas and asparagus is the coating for soft-boiled eggs in this recipe. Lovely summery food, best served with rice and a tossed salad – and some warm, fresh bread on the side.

Plunge the boiled eggs into cold water as soon as the four minutes are up. When they are cold, peel very carefully, making sure not to break the white. Purée the peas and the asparagus together with the melted margarine and béchamel – the purée should be smooth and a lovely shade of green. Thin out with a little single cream and season to taste. Divide the mixture into the bottom of two ramekin dishes. Put the eggs on top and garnish with a sprig of parsley. Serve at room temperature.

Spicy Eggs

Serves 2

Butter or sunflower margarine, 25 g (1 oz)

2 spring onions, finely sliced

Garam masala, 1 tsp

2 tomatoes, skinned and very finely chopped

Turmeric, 1–2 tsp

3 eggs, beaten

Salt and pepper

Coriander leaves to garnish

This is a kind of scrambled eggs 'Indian Style': a stir-fry of spring onions and tomatoes is flavoured with garam masala and turmeric, and then the eggs are scrambled into the mixture. Lovely with chapatis and a mixed salad.

Melt the butter or margarine in a heavy-bottomed saucepan and soften the spring onions over a gentle heat for 4–5 minutes. Then add the garam masala and the chopped tomatoes and cook for a further 3–4 minutes. Season with the turmeric, salt and pepper and mix well, then pour in the eggs and begin to scramble them, stirring with a fork. When the eggs are lightly set but still moist – not dry and overcooked – serve at once on warm plates with a mixed salad and chapatis, garnished with fresh coriander leaves.

To skin tomatoes

Put the tomatoes into a bowl and cover with boiling water. Leave to stand for 3–4 minutes, then the skin will peel off easily with a sharp knife.

Eggs Soubise

Serves 2

4 eggs, lightly poached

Soubise sauce (see below),
300 ml (½ pint)

Triangles of fried bread

Soubise sauce

Rice, 50 g (2 oz) washed

Vegetable stock, 450 ml
(¾ pint)

Onions, 175 g (6 oz)
sliced finely

Butter or margarine, 25 g
(1 oz)

Cream or yogurt to finish
(optional)

Salt and pepper

This recipe for soubise sauce comes from a French chef who bases it on a classic method. The addition of rice to the sauce gives it bulk and a satisfying baseline, perfect for lightly poached eggs. Served with triangles of fried bread, this dish makes an excellent supper.

To make the soubise sauce, start by cooking the rice for 5 minutes in salted boiling water. Drain. Heat the stock to boiling-point, and put in the onions and the rice. Simmer for 30 minutes until well reduced, stirring from time to time. Add the butter or margarine, purée in the

blender, reheat, then thin out with a little cream or yogurt. Check the seasoning and serve hot.

Place each poached egg in a warm ramekin dish and spoon some soubise sauce over them. Surround with crisp, golden triangles of fried bread and serve immediately.

Artichoke Frittata

Serves 2

2 shallots, finely sliced

Unsalted butter or margarine, 15 g (½ oz)

Jerusalem artichokes, 225 g (8 oz) cooked and sliced

3 large eggs, lightly beaten

Fresh basil, 1 tsp finely chopped

Fresh parsley, 2 tbs finely chopped

Parmesan, 2 tbs freshly grated

Salt and pepper

A frittata is a kind of omelette, cooked more slowly and with more of a filling. This one, with Jerusalem artichokes and herbs, makes cold-weather food *par excellence*. Serve it with a potato dish, or rice, and a crunchy salad.

Cook the shallots in the butter over a low heat, stirring, until they have softened. Add the artichokes, and stir to coat them with the butter. In a bowl combine the eggs, basil, parsley, 1 tbs of the Parmesan, and salt and pepper to taste. Pour the mixture into a large, heavy pan, add the shallots and artichokes, and cook the frittata over a moderately low heat, without stirring, until the edges are golden but the centre is still unset. Sprinkle the top with the remaining Parmesan and put it under a preheated grill for 1–2 minutes, until it is just set. Cut into wedges and transfer it to heated plates.

You can also make this with salsify. As good cold as hot.

Poached Eggs with Garlic Mushrooms

Serves 2

Small button mushrooms,
75 g (3 oz) sliced

Butter or sunflower
margarine, 25 g (1 oz)

1 clove of garlic, crushed

Parsley, 2 tbs finely
chopped

Vegetable stock, 4 tbs

2 eggs, lightly poached

Salt and pepper

Nothing is more delicious than mush-rooms cooked in butter with garlic and parsley – so simple, yet unbeatable. As a topping for poached eggs they come into their own as a wonderful light meal at any time of the year.

Sauté the mushrooms in the butter or sun-flower margarine until lightly cooked, then stir in the garlic and parsley and cook gently for a further 2–3 minutes. Season with a little salt and pepper and add the stock. Heat through. Place the eggs in separate ramekin dishes and spoon the mushroom mixture over the top. Serve at once with warm granary bread and a crisp salad.

Kookoo

Serves 2–3

Vegetable oil, 2 tbs

Medium potatoes, 350 g
(12 oz) peeled and very
finely sliced

Mushrooms, 100 g (4 oz)
minced in the blender

3 spring onions, finely
chopped

Parsley, 2 tbs finely
chopped

3 eggs, beaten

Salt and pepper

Cheddar, finely grated, to
garnish

A delightful name for a delightful dish. Kookoo makes a substantial and satisfying meal in its own right, served with just a side-salad.

Grease a large, heavy frying-pan with 2 tsp of the oil and arrange the sliced pota-toes over the surface. Season with a little salt and pepper and dribble the rest of the oil over them. Cover with a lid and cook over a very gentle heat for 10 minutes.

Mix the mushrooms, spring onions and parsley into the beaten eggs and season to taste. Pour over the potatoes in the pan, cover again and cook over a low heat for a further 10 minutes.

Slide the kookoo out of the pan on to a platter and serve it cut in wedges. Hand around grated cheese to sprinkle over the top.

Crêpes à la Pipérade

Serves 3

For 9–10 cm (4 inch) crêpes

Flour, 40 g (1½ oz)

1 egg

Salt, ¼ tsp

Vegetable oil, 1 tsp

Milk, 50 ml (2 fl. oz)

Onions, 175 g (6 oz) finely sliced

Vegetable oil, 2 tbs

Green pepper, 175 g (6 oz) de-seeded and sliced

2 ripe tomatoes, skinned (p. 67) and chopped

2 cloves of garlic, crushed

Parsley, 1 tbs chopped

Fresh basil leaves, 1 tbs chopped

Gruyère cheese, 50 g (2 oz) diced very small

Salt and pepper

These little crêpes are made with a French country recipe for onions, peppers and tomatoes cooked with garlic, basil and parsley. The pipérade mixture is folded into the pancake batter and the crêpes are cooked until golden. Lovely with a tossed green salad.

Blend the ingredients for the crêpe batter together and allow to rest for an hour.

Cook the onions gently in the oil for about 10 minutes, covered, stirring occasionally until soft and sweet. Add the sliced peppers and cook for a further 5 minutes. Add the chopped tomatoes and garlic and cover the pan for several minutes, until the mixture is well reduced. Continue to cook over a slightly raised heat for 5 minutes, adding the herbs and stirring the mixture thoroughly. Season to taste. Add the cheese to the pipérade mixture and stir into the crêpe batter. Fry in a hot pan with a little oil, as for ordinary crêpes, turning so that they cook until golden on both sides.

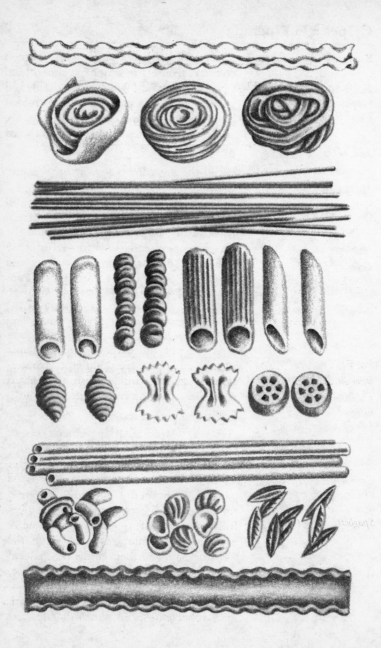

PASTA AND NOODLES

Spaghetti with Garlic Croûtons and Fresh Tomato Sauce

Serves 2

For the sauce

Olive oil, 2 tbs

1 medium onion, finely sliced

1 clove of garlic, crushed

Fresh mixed herbs, 2 tbs finely chopped

Canned tomatoes, 400 g (14 oz)

Spaghetti, 175 g (6 oz) cooked 'al dente'

Salt and pepper

Garlic croûtons (see p. 37) and grated cheese to garnish

A home-made tomato sauce, with the freshness of herbs and garlic, is an unbeatable rival to any commercial variety. This version of a classic spaghetti dish is sprinkled with garlic croûtons and is utterly mouth-watering.

Heat the oil in a large pan and gently cook the onion in it, stirring until it softens but not allowing it to brown. After about 6–7 minutes, stir in the crushed garlic and the herbs, and cook together for a further 5 minutes. Add the juices from the can of tomatoes and simmer together for 5 minutes more. Chop the tomatoes and add them to the pan, season to taste, and pour the sauce over the hot, drained spaghetti. Top with garlic croûtons. Serve at once, on warm plates, with grated cheese to sprinkle over the top.

Pasta with Courgette Sauce

Serves 2

3 medium courgettes

Olive oil, 3 tbs

1 clove of garlic, crushed

Fresh tagliatelle, 225 g
(8 oz) (or 175 g (6 oz)
dried)

Vinaigrette, 50 ml
(2 fl. oz)

Salt and pepper

Chopped chives and grated
cheese to garnish

A simple purée of steamed courgettes and garlic is all that this sauce is – and it is wonderful. The flavours are lovely, the colour is fresh green. Serve this dish with a tossed salad and some fresh bread.

Steam the courgettes until tender, about 5 minutes. Cool, chop them, then put in the liquidizer and blend to a purée with the olive oil. Season to taste with garlic, salt and pepper.

Cook the pasta in boiling, salted water until *al dente*, then drain well. Toss the vinaigrette into the warm pasta and serve on warm plates. Spoon the courgette sauce over the top and garnish with chopped chives. Sprinkle grated cheese over the top.

Tagliatelle with Chinese Vegetables

Serves 2–3

3 spring onions, sliced

Fresh root ginger, 2.5 cm
(1 inch) grated

Dark sesame oil, 3 tbs

Baby sweetcorn, 75 g
(3 oz) sliced

Water-chestnuts, 50 g
(2 oz) sliced

Button mushrooms, 75 g
(3 oz) quartered

Mange-tout, 50 g (2 oz)
sliced diagonally

Soy sauce, 2 tbs

Tagliatelle, 175 g (6 oz)
cooked 'al dente'

This is a kind of western chow mein, quickly and easily prepared. A delicious way to eat tagliatelle, the soft pasta contrasting with the crunchiness of the Chinese vegetables.

Stir-fry the spring onions and ginger gently in the oil for a couple of minutes so that they soften, then toss in the prepared vegetables and stir until they heat through and begin to soften – about 4–5 minutes. Then stir in the soy sauce and heat through again, stirring all the time. Pour this mixture over the hot, drained tagliatelle in a warm serving-dish, toss thoroughly and serve immediately.

Linguini in Spicy Sauce

Serves 2

Vegetable oil, 3 tbs

1 clove of garlic, crushed

Garam masala, 1 tbs

Turmeric, 1 tsp

Chinese leaf, 100 g (4 oz) finely shredded

Vegetable stock, 5 tbs

Yogurt, 3 tbs

Linguini, 175 g (6 oz) cooked 'al dente'

Salt

For those who love hot spices, this dish of linguini with garam masala and garlic, and shredded Chinese leaf, makes a refreshing change from blander pasta dishes. Serve this one with a tomato and onion salad and some hot nan bread.

Heat the oil gently and fry the garlic, garam masala and turmeric together for a few minutes. Then stir in the Chinese leaves and stir-fry until they soften. Add the stock, heat through and season with a little salt. Then mix in the yogurt, and when the sauce is smooth and even pour over the hot, drained linguini and toss thoroughly. Serve at once, on hot plates.

Fettucine with Mushrooms and Cream

Serves 2

1 small onion, finely sliced

Olive oil, 2 tbs

Dried mixed herbs, 1 tsp

Mushrooms, 100 g (4 oz) sliced

Single cream, 5 tbs

Fettucine, 175 g (6 oz) cooked 'al dente'

1 egg, beaten

Salt and pepper

Grated Parmesan to garnish

Classic Mediterranean food, a creamy mushroom sauce is folded into freshly cooked fettucine, and an egg lightly scrambled into the mixture at the last moment until it is lightly set. Serve this with a garlicky green salad and some warm granary bread.

Simmer the sliced onion gently in the oil until thoroughly softened, then add the herbs and let them soften too, stirring. Add the mushrooms and stir them until their juices start to run. Stir the cream into the mixture and heat through. Pour the sauce over the hot, drained fettucine in a saucepan, and put over a very gentle heat. Finally add the beaten egg and cook slowly, stirring, until the egg begins to set. Check the seasoning and serve at once on warm plates. Sprinkle grated Parmesan over the top.

Rice Noodles Oriental-style

Serves 2

Rice noodles, 175 g (6 oz)

2 medium courgettes, thinly sliced diagonally

Broccoli florets, 100 g (4 oz) sliced thinly

Okra, 100 g (4 oz) topped and tailed

Dark sesame oil, 2 tbs

1 clove of garlic, crushed

Fresh root ginger, 1 cm (½ inch) grated

Soy sauce, 1–2 tbs

Rice noodles make a delightful alternative to wheat-based noodles – fine in texture, they are light food that is quickly cooked and make a delicious base for all kinds of mixtures. Here chopped courgettes, broccoli and okra are flavoured with ginger, garlic and soy sauce: irresistible food.

Cook the rice noodles in boiling water until they are soft, about 3–4 minutes. Drain.

Steam the finely sliced courgettes, broccoli and okra al dente. Heat the oil and quickly stir in all the vegetables until they are coated with it, then mix in the garlic and ginger. Season with the soy sauce and mix together thoroughly. Toss the cooked rice noodles into the pan, stir-fry for a further minute or two until they are well coated, and serve immediately.

Crunchy Chinese Noodles

Serves 2

Egg noodles, 125 g (5 oz)

Dark sesame oil, 2 tbs

Root ginger, 2.5 cm (1 inch) finely grated

1 clove of garlic, crushed

Soy sauce, 1–2 tbs

3 spring onions, finely sliced

Pine nuts, 25 g (1 oz) browned under the grill

Fresh coriander leaves to garnish

The crunch of browned pine nuts gives this simple mixture of egg noodles, garlic and ginger a mouth-watering texture. The dish is made in a matter of moments, and a finishing touch of fresh coriander makes all the difference, adding its distinctively oriental flavour.

Cook the egg noodles in boiling, salted water until soft – about 4–5 minutes. Heat the oil in a wok and soften the ginger and garlic gently in it for 3–4 minutes, then toss in the noodles until well coated. Stir in the soy sauce and spring onions and cook for another 3–4 minutes. Finally stir in the pine nuts and mix thoroughly. Serve immediately, garnished with fresh coriander leaves.

Tagliatelle with Mange-tout

Serves 2

Mange-tout, 175 g (6 oz)
cut diagonally

1 shallot, sliced

Olive oil, 2 tbs

1 clove of garlic, crushed

Single cream, 5 tbs

Fresh tagliatelle, 225 g
(8 oz) cooked 'al dente'

Parmesan, grated

Pepper to taste

Crisp mange-tout are stir-fried with garlic and shallot and finished with cream, making an appetizing sauce for fresh tagliatelle. Sprinkled generously with cheese, the dish is then quickly browned under the grill. All it needs is a tossed green salad to go with it.

Steam the sliced mange-tout until tender but still crisp, about 2–3 minutes. Soften the shallot in the oil and add the garlic. Stir in the prepared mange-tout and season to taste with pepper. Add the cream and heat through, stirring. Then toss the tagliatelle into the sauce and put in a heatproof dish. Sprinkle with the grated Parmesan and brown under a hot grill for a minute or less, then serve at once.

Spicy Beansprouts with Vermicelli

Serves 2

3 spring onions, sliced

Dark sesame oil, 2 tbs

Garam masala, 1 tsp

1 clove of garlic, crushed

Beansprouts, 100 g (4 oz)

Vermicelli, 150 g (5 oz)

Chopped coriander to
garnish, 1 tbs

So quick to make, this dish has all the qualities of classic Eastern cookery. Chopped coriander, sprinkled over it just before serving, is the finishing touch.

Soften the spring onions in the oil for a few minutes and then add the garam masala and garlic. Stir for another minute or so and then toss in the beansprouts and stir-fry for another 3–4 minutes until heated through, tender but still crisp. Cook and drain the vermicelli and add to the pan, stirring until well mixed and hot. Serve in a warm dish, sprinkled with the fresh chopped coriander.

Spaghetti Soubise

Serves 2

2 large onions, finely
chopped

Olive oil, 2 tbs

Crème fraîche or thick set
yogurt, 75 g (3 oz)

Spaghetti, 175 g (6 oz)

Parmesan, 25 g (1 oz)
grated

Salt and freshly ground
black pepper

A simple sauce of sweated onions, sweet
and soft, goes really well on spaghetti.
Lots of freshly ground black pepper,
Parmesan, and some crème fraîche or
yogurt make it a memorable dish.

Cook the onions in the olive oil over a
very gentle heat, covered, for 30 minutes,
stirring from time to time until they are
soft, transparent and sweet but not
browned. Season with a little salt and lots
of freshly ground black pepper. Cool a
little, then stir in the crème fraîche.

Meanwhile cook the spaghetti *al dente*
and drain it. Pour the sauce over the top
and toss well together. Serve with the
grated cheese.

Weekend Tagliatelle

Serves 2

1–2 large cloves of garlic,
crushed

Olive oil, 2 tbs

Fresh tagliatelle, 175 g
(6 oz) cooked 'al dente'

Pine nuts, 40 g (1½ oz)
lightly browned

Freshly ground black
pepper

You have to eat this at the weekend simply
because it is so incredibly garlicky as to be
anti-social to anyone who has not eaten it!
For all its simplicity, it is among the most
delicious of pasta dishes.

Stir the crushed garlic into the olive oil
and add masses of freshly ground black
pepper. Mix into the hot, drained tagliatelle and toss thoroughly. Finally mix in
the pine nuts, give it all another toss and
serve immediately with a crisp green
salad.

Spinach Fettucine

Serves 2

1 clove of garlic, finely chopped

Unsalted butter, 40 g (1½ oz)

Cooked spinach, 150 g (5 oz) finely chopped

Fresh green fettucine, 225 g (8 oz) cooked 'al dente'

Parmesan, 2 tbs grated

Roquefort, 50 g (2 oz) crumbled

Crème fraîche, 75 g (3 oz)

Salt and pepper

Spinach goes particularly well with pasta, and especially so with green pasta, with which it has an obvious affinity. This lovely sauce of spinach with blue cheese and crème fraîche makes a memorable and substantial meal. Serve it with a crisp green salad and some fresh bread for the juices on the plate.

Soften the garlic in the butter over a gentle heat, stirring. Add the spinach and mix well. Toss in the cooked fettucine and coat it with the mixture. Add the cheeses and the crème fraîche, and season to taste with salt and pepper. Heat through, tossing well, until the cheeses have melted. Divide the mixture between two warmed plates.

Vegetable Noodles Malay-style

Serves 2–3

Small okra, 100 g (4 oz)

Baby courgettes, 100 g (4 oz) thinly sliced

Egg noodles, 225 g (8 oz)

Dark sesame oil, 2 tbs

1 clove of garlic, crushed

½ a small fresh chilli, finely chopped

2 spring onions, sliced

Black-bean sauce, 1 tbs

Beansprouts, 100 g (4 oz)

1 small bunch of chives, chopped

Coriander leaves to garnish

A wonderful medley of interesting vegetables, some egg noodles, and oriental flavours of black bean, sesame, garlic and chilli. This is blissful food at any time of the year.

Steam the vegetables until tender and set aside. Cook the egg noodles for 4–5 minutes in boiling, salted water, stirring occasionally. Drain. Heat the oil and quickly stir-fry the garlic, chilli and spring onions. Stir in the black-bean sauce. Add the noodles to the pan and toss in the mixture, then add all the vegetables and the chives, and stir-fry until they are heated through and tender, but still slightly crisp. Serve at once, garnished with coriander leaves.

Fresh Pasta with Peas

Serves 2–3

Olive oil, 2 tbs

½ a yellow pepper, finely chopped

Peas, 100 g (4 oz) cooked

Fresh pasta ribbons, 225 g (8 oz)

Butter, 25 g (1 oz) softened

Crème fraîche, 50 g (2 oz)

Parmesan, 25 g (1 oz)

Freshly ground pepper

The tang of pepper gives this gentle pasta dish a distinctive touch. The creaminess of crème fraîche, some Parmesan, freshly ground black pepper – and you have a delicious supper dish.

Heat the oil and gently fry the yellow pepper for a few minutes. Add the peas, mix well and season with pepper. Cover and leave to cook over a very low heat for 15 minutes, until well softened.

Cook the pasta *al dente* and drain it. Put it into a warm dish and pour the pepper and pea mixture over it. Add the butter, crème fraîche and Parmesan. Toss well and serve immediately.

Penne with Cauliflower

Serves 2–3

1 small cauliflower, divided
into florets

1 onion, finely chopped

Olive oil, 4 tbs

Raisins, 25 g (1 oz)
soaked in hot water for
20 minutes

Pine nuts, 50 g (2 oz)
toasted

Penne, 175 g (6 oz)
cooked 'al dente'

Cheddar, 25 g (1 oz)
grated

Parsley, 1 tbs finely
chopped to garnish

Salt and pepper to taste

An unusual combination of tastes makes
this a pasta dish with a difference – raisins
and pine nuts give it a quite distinctive
quality. Serve it with a tossed green salad.

Steam the cauliflower florets *al dente*. Cut
them into thin slices. Sauté the onion in
the oil over a moderate heat until it begins
to brown. Simmer, partially covered, for
5 minutes. Stir in the raisins, pine nuts
and cauliflower and season to taste with
salt and pepper.

Toss the cooked penne with half of the
sauce and spoon the rest over the top.
Sprinkle the dish with the grated cheese
and garnish with the parsley. Serve hot,
on warmed plates.

PASTA SALADS

There is no end to the variety of salads that you can make using pasta shapes as a base. Improvisation is the name of the game – selecting fresh vegetables and chopping them finely to toss into the cooked, cooled pasta. Dress the salad while it is still warm – you will need lots of dressing since the pasta soaks it up greedily! Some of the best pasta salads are made with avocado, mushrooms either raw or lightly steamed, grilled peppers, carrots and cucumber, French beans and mange-tout, Feta cheese, fresh summer herbs, cauliflower – a kaleidoscope of good things.

Pasta Bows Special Salad

Serves 2–3

Pasta bows, 225 g (8 oz) cooked 'al dente'

3 medium courgettes, finely diced

1 canned pimento, finely chopped

Fresh tarragon, 2 tbs chopped

For the dressing
Olive oil, 4–5 tbs

Raspberry vinegar (see p. 121), 1 tbs

1–2 cloves of garlic, crushed

Pasta salads make wonderful meals through all the seasons of the year. This one is dressed with a lovely mixture of olive oil, raspberry vinegar and garlic, which soaks into the cooled pasta, making it special indeed.

Rinse the cooked, drained pasta bows under running water and shake them dry. Mix them with the courgettes, pimento and chopped tarragon.

Stir the olive oil, raspberry vinegar and garlic together and dress the salad with the mixture. Leave to stand for an hour or so for the pasta to soak up the dressing.

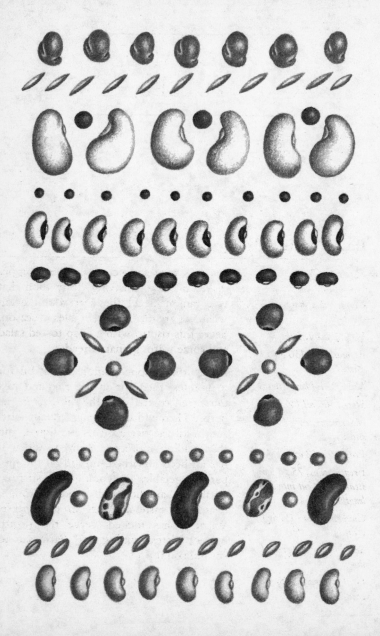

RICE AND
PULSES

Best Risotto

Serves 2–3

1 large onion, finely chopped

Vegetable oil, 3 tbs

Basmati rice, 150 g (5 oz) washed

Mixed dried herbs, 1 tbs

Stock, 300 ml (½ pint)

Mushrooms, 75 g (3 oz) sliced

Peas, 50 g (2 oz) cooked

French beans, 75 g (3 oz) steamed and cut into short lengths

Cheddar, 40 g (1½ oz) grated

Salt, pepper and ground mace

Grated Parmesan to garnish

Risottos make some of the best supper dishes of all – satisfying, tasty food that you can make all the year round using whatever are the best vegetables in season. Serve this risotto with a crisp tossed salad and some warm granary bread.

Soften the chopped onion in the oil for 5 minutes, then stir in the rice and mix until well coated with the oil. Stir in the herbs. Then add the stock gradually, stirring until the rice absorbs the liquid, and then adding more as required. When it has all been absorbed, mix in all the prepared vegetables and cook gently, stirring, until they are hot and cooked through. Season to taste and stir in the cheese. When it has melted, serve the risotto on hot plates, with grated Parmesan to sprinkle on top.

Spiced Lentils with Cauliflower

Serves 2–3

Red lentils, 100 g (4 oz) washed

Garam masala, 2 tsp

½ a fresh green chilli, finely chopped

1 clove of garlic, crushed

1 small onion, finely sliced

Turmeric, ½ tsp

Coconut milk (see p. 54), 300 ml (½ pint)

½ a medium cauliflower, cut into small florets

1 large tomato, skinned (see p. 67) and chopped

Yogurt, 100 g (4 oz)

Salt to taste

This version of dhal with cauliflower is nothing short of brilliant: beautiful gentle spices, lovely textures, and amazing tastes that linger on the palate. Serve it with basmati rice, warm chapatis and a green salad.

Drain the lentils and put into a pan with the garam masala, chilli, crushed garlic, sliced onion and turmeric. Cover with the coconut milk and simmer for 12–15 minutes, until tender and soft. Add the cauliflower and tomato and simmer for a further 10 minutes. Stir in the yogurt and heat through. Season to taste with salt.

Four-cheese Rice

Serves 2

Long-grain rice, 100 g (4 oz)

Water, 75 ml (3 fl. oz)

Mozzarella, 40 g (1½ oz) sliced

Bel Paese, 40 g (1½ oz) diced small

Gruyère, 40 g (1½ oz) grated

Parmesan, 1 tbs grated

Mixed dried herbs, 1 tsp

1 egg, well beaten

Salt and pepper

Substantial, warming food for cold weather, this dish is rich and nourishing. Gorgeous with a mixed salad dressed with a garlicky vinaigrette.

Cover the rice with the water and bring to the boil. Then cover with a lid and simmer until all the water is absorbed, about 8–10 minutes. Stir it to fluff it up, then toss in all the cheeses and the herbs. Season to taste with salt and pepper. Finally fold in the beaten egg and put the dish in a pre-heated oven at 220°C/425°F/ gas 7 for 8–10 minutes. Serve very hot.

Kitchri with Peas

Serves 2–3

Basmati rice, 75 g (3 oz)
washed

Green lentils, 50 g (2 oz)
washed

Butter or sunflower
margarine, 25 g (1 oz)

1 small onion, thinly sliced

Fresh root ginger, 1 cm
(½ inch) grated

1 clove of garlic, crushed

Chilli powder, 1 tsp

Water, 300 ml (½ pint)

Peas, 75 g (3 oz) cooked

Salt

Kitchri is an Indian recipe, a satisfying and wholesome mixture of rice and lentils lightly spiced with ginger and chilli. Adding a few peas to this mixture turns it into a meal in itself.

Drain the washed rice and lentils. Melt the margarine or butter and sauté the onion, ginger, garlic and chilli in it until the onion is lightly browned. Add the rice and the lentils and stir-fry for a minute or two. Pour in the water and add a little salt. Bring to the boil, reduce the heat and simmer gently for 20 minutes. Serve with the cooked peas.

Dhal

Serves 2–3

Green or brown lentils,
175 g (6 oz)

2 small onions, chopped
small

Fresh root ginger, 5 cm
(2 inches) bruised

Ground coriander, 2 tbs

Ground cumin, 2 tsp

Ground ginger, 2 tsp

Salt

A classic dhal takes a lot of beating. This recipe came from an Indian friend and has become a firmly established favourite. Serve it with some plain rice, chapatis and a crisp salad – and you have a meal in a million.

Soak the lentils for 6 hours or over-night. Drain, put them into a saucepan and cover with fresh cold water. Add the onion and root ginger. Bring to the boil and simmer for 20 minutes, until the lentils are tender. Remove the root ginger. Add a little salt and leave to cool in the cooking water. After 10 minutes or so stir in the ground spices and leave until cold. This dhal is best the next day, served gently re-heated.

Pease Pudding

Serves 3–4

Split peas, 225 g (8 oz)
soaked for 6 hours

1 small onion, chopped

1 medium carrot, sliced

1 turnip, peeled and sliced

1 stalk of celery, sliced

2 egg yolks, well beaten

Butter or margarine, 15 g
(½ oz)

Fresh mixed herbs, e.g.
chives, marjoram, parsley,
lovage, 2 tbs freshly
chopped

Salt and pepper

A nursery favourite, pease pudding makes a marvellous meal when it is well flavoured with herbs and cooked so that it remains moist. Nourishing, warming food that goes well with an interesting salad or two of your choice (see 'Composite Salads', p. 95).

Drain the split peas and cover with water in a saucepan. Add the vegetables and simmer all together until tender, about 45 minutes, adding more boiling water as the peas soak up the water. When they are soft, drain off most of the water and liquidize the peas to a purée. Stir in the egg yolks and butter or margarine. Add the

herbs and season to taste. Put the mixture into a greased pudding basin, cover with foil or a lid, or both if possible, and steam over hot water for 35–40 minutes or until firmly set. Cool for 5–10 minutes, then turn out on to a serving-dish.

Saffron Rice

Serves 2

Saffron threads, ¼ tsp

Hot milk, 1 tbs

Basmati rice, 100 g (4 oz) washed

Water, 150 ml (¼ pint)

Salt

A classic recipe from Middle Eastern cookery, this is hard to beat for a simple side-dish to go with a spicy meal. The rice takes on the delicate gold colour of saffron, and its subtle, inimitable flavour permeates the dish – a treat.

Soak the saffron threads in the milk. Cook the rice in the water, covered for about 8–10 minutes until soft but not mushy. It should absorb all the water. Stir in the saffron mixture and stir until the rice takes on a golden colour. Add a little salt to taste. Put into a warm dish and it is ready to serve.

Fragrant Fried Rice

Serves 2

Ground turmeric, 1 tsp

5-spice, 1 tsp

Sunflower oil, 2 tbs

Long-grain rice, 175 g (6 oz) cooked

Salt

Browned pine nuts to garnish

Simplicity itself, the aromatic spicing of turmeric and five-spice transforms rice both in colour and in flavour. The golden dish is finally garnished with browned pine nuts, which add their irresistible crunch to the soft rice.

Simmer the spices in the oil for 2–3 minutes, then add to the drained rice and toss well. When well mixed together and heated through, season to taste, separate the grains with a fork and serve garnished with the browned pine nuts.

Rice Layers

Serves 2–3

½ a medium cauliflower, steamed until tender

Mushrooms, 175 g (6 oz) sliced

Olive oil, 2–3 tbs

Rice, 225 g (8 oz) cooked

Mustard and cheese sauce (see p. 119), 300 ml (½ pint)

Breadcrumbs, 2 tbs

Cheddar, 2 tbs grated

A little butter or margarine

This sumptuous dish is a great favourite – layers of cauliflower, mushrooms and rice are covered with a mustard and cheese sauce and then browned in the oven. Serve with a mixed salad of your choice and some warm bread to mop up the juices.

Slice the cauliflower finely. Sauté the mushrooms briskly in hot olive oil until cooked through but still crisp. Make a layer of the cauliflower in the bottom of a small, greased serving-dish, and cover with a layer of rice. Continue with a layer of the mushrooms, and so on, until the ingredients are used up. Cover with the sauce. Mix together the breadcrumbs and grated cheese and sprinkle over the top. Dot with butter or margarine and bake at 190°C/375°F/gas 5 for 20 minutes.

Rice Salad with Olives

Serves 2

Long-grain rice, 75 g (3 oz)

Wild rice, 25 g (1 oz)

White-wine vinegar, 2 tbs

Olive oil, 4 tbs

8 pimento-stuffed green olives

Spring onions, 40 g (1½ oz) finely chopped

Parsley, 3 tbs finely chopped

Salt and pepper

Rice salads, like risottos (see p. 85), can be made through all the seasons of the year using fresh vegetables of your choice. This one is very simply made with olives, spring onions and parsley, and dressed with oil and vinegar. Lovely as part of a cold table with a variety of salads to go with it.

Cook the two rices separately, as instructed on the packets (and see p. 42). Whisk together the vinegar with the oil, and season with salt and pepper. Dress the warm rice with the mixture. Toss in the stuffed olives, spring onions and parsley and mix well. Leave at room temperature for a few hours so that the flavours can amalgamate before serving.

Pineapple Rice Salad

Serves 2–3

For the dressing
Yogurt, 100 g (4 oz)

Sour cream, 2 tbs

Mint leaves, 2 tbs finely
chopped

Garam masala, 2 tsp

Salt and pepper

Rice, 150 g (5 oz) cooked

Pineapple, 225 g (8 oz)
cubed small

½ a cucumber, peeled and
diced

Spring onions, 40 g
(1½ oz) finely chopped

4 radishes, finely sliced

Soft-leaved lettuce for lining
the platter

This rice salad is for special occasions – a lovely mixture of pineapple, cucumber, spring onions and radishes mingles with the rice, and all are dressed in a minty yogurt dressing.

To make the dressing, in a bowl combine the yogurt, sour cream, mint, garam masala, and salt and pepper to taste.

In another bowl combine the rice, pineapple, cucumber, spring onion and radishes, and season to taste with salt and pepper. Toss the salad with the dressing and let it stand, covered, for 30 minutes. Line a platter with the lettuce and mound the rice salad into the centre.

Rice with Pesto Sauce

Serves 2–3

Long-grain rice, 150 g
(5 oz) washed

Sunflower oil, 1 tbs

Pesto sauce, 3 tbs
(see p. 120)

Salt and pepper

Grated Gruyère

Quick, cheap and easy – this recipe fits all those bills! It is deceptively good, too, for all its simplicity. Serve it with a tossed salad and some warm granary rolls.

Put the rice into a large saucepan of boiling salted water, add the oil (to prevent it sticking), and simmer for about 8–10 minutes, until well cooked. Drain and pile into a serving-dish. Spoon the pesto sauce over the top, stir in well and season to taste. Serve with a bowl of finely grated Gruyère to sprinkle over it.

Flageolets with Pesto

Serves 2

Canned flageolets, 400 g (14 oz)

Pesto sauce (see p. 120), 2–3 tbs

Small button mushrooms, 75 g (3 oz) finely sliced

This is a fantastic salad, prepared in no time at all, and at very little cost. Serve it with warm nan bread and one or two other interesting salads (see 'Composite Salads', p. 95).

Drain the flageolets and reserve a little of the liquid. Mix the pesto with 1 tbs of the liquid, adding more if necessary to bring to a mayonnaise consistency. Dress the flageolets in the pesto mixture, and fold in the mushrooms. Mix well. Leave to stand at room temperature for an hour or two before serving. Heap on to soft lettuce leaves lightly dressed with vinaigrette and serve.

Kasha

Serves 2–3

Sunflower oil, 3 tbs

Buckwheat, 175 g (6 oz)

Water, 450 ml (¾ pint)

Butter or sunflower margarine, 50 g (2 oz)

Large bunch of chopped fresh herbs

1 egg, beaten

Cheddar, 75 g (3 oz) grated

Based on a traditional Russian recipe, this dish is made with buckwheat, cheese and herbs. Rustic food indeed, a nourishing and satisfying supper dish which is delightful served with a composite salad of your choice (see p. 95).

Heat the oil gently in a saucepan and toss the buckwheat in it until it begins to brown and becomes fragrant. When well browned, pour in the water, and bring to simmering-point. Simmer gently for 15–20 minutes, until tender. Leave to cool – it will absorb the liquid, so do not drain it. After 10–15 minutes stir in the butter or margarine and the herbs, and cool. Fold in the beaten egg, and make layers of this mixture with the grated cheese in a well-greased baking-dish. Cover with a layer of the cheese and bake at 170°C/325°F/gas 3 for 25 minutes.

COOKING WITH
LEFTOVERS

Improvisation with leftovers can be one of the most rewarding areas of eating alone or *à deux*. You can never repeat yourself, and it is surprising what ingredients combine to make memorable meals. Leftover potatoes with the remains of an aubergine dish; courgettes with a mushroom recipe – both could work very well. Mix leftover main courses either together, with side-vegetables, or with some leftover pasta. Pep up leftover rice or pulses with mixed vegetables or with a leftover egg dish, chopped up.

Always keep leftover food refrigerated and covered with plastic film to keep it as fresh as possible. To reheat, put the reconstituted meal into a suitable dish, cover with a suitable film-wrap, and microwave for the appropriate time – just long enough for it to heat through without over-cooking it. If you don't use a microwave, you can reheat it either in a steamer or in a conventional oven, well wrapped in foil to keep it moist. The principal hazard is over-heating and allowing the food to dry out. In this respect the microwave gives the best results, since the food is effectively steamed. A traditional steamer will take longer but also gives good results.

COMPOSITE
SALADS

You can make complete meals from composite salads, meals which are healthy and satisfying, yet light and enjoyable to prepare. The possibilities of salads have increased greatly with the appearance of wonderful – and unseasonal – produce on the supermarket shelf in recent years, and in many cases the salads that you prepare can be a meal in themselves, served with warm granary bread and butter. They make interesting side-salads with a difference, too.

Oriental Salad

Serves 2–3

Canned sweetcorn, 225 g (8 oz) drained

Beansprouts, 50 g (2 oz)

Small button mushrooms, 50 g (2 oz) quartered

2 canned pimentos, drained and chopped

Rice, 50 g (2 oz) cooked and drained

Root ginger, 1 cm (½ inch) grated

Soy sauce, 1–2 tbs

Vinaigrette, 3 tbs

Mix all the prepared vegetables and the rice together. Stir the grated ginger into the soy sauce and mix with the vinaigrette. Dress the salad with this mixture and put into a bowl. Leave for a few hours in a cool place so that the flavours have a chance to blend.

Autumn Salad

Serves 2–3

*Cooked marrow, 225 g
(8 oz) skinned and cubed*

*2 large tomatoes, skinned
(see p. 67) and chopped*

1 large carrot, grated

*Blackberries, 75 g (3 oz)
washed and hulled*

*Cooked beetroot, 100 g
(4 oz) skinned and diced
small*

Tahini paste, 1 tbs

Mayonnaise, 5 tbs

1 clove of garlic, crushed

*Freshly ground black
pepper*

Combine the marrow, tomatoes, carrot, blackberries and beetroot and mix thoroughly. Stir the tahini paste into the mayonnaise and add the crushed garlic. Season the dressing with freshly ground black pepper and fold into the prepared vegetables. Place on top of a bed of shredded lettuce and the salad is ready to serve.

Mixed-dish Salad

Serves 2

*1 crisp lettuce, trimmed
and washed*

1 celery heart

1 orange, peeled and sliced

*Hard cheese, 50 g (2 oz)
cubed*

*Croûtons (see p. 37),
2 tbs*

Parmesan, 1 tbs grated

*Garlic mayonnaise (see
p. 122), 3 tbs*

Place the lettuce leaves in the bottom, and around the edge, of two wooden bowls. Slice the celery lengthwise and place in a radiating pattern on top. Cut the orange slices into quarters and put them in the centre. Mix the cubed cheese with the croûtons and sprinkle over, then sprinkle with the grated Parmesan. Dribble garlic mayonnaise over the top in a lattice pattern and the salad is ready to serve.

Watercress, Peach and Raisin Salad

Serves 2

*1 small bunch watercress,
washed and trimmed*

*1 large peach, skinned and
stoned*

Raisins, 40 g (1½ oz)

*1 medium crisp lettuce,
trimmed, washed and
shredded*

*A few radicchio leaves,
torn into small pieces*

*Orange vinaigrette (see
p. 121), 3 tbs*

Chop the watercress and cut the peaches
into small cubes. Combine all the ingredients and dress in the orange vinaigrette.

Gherkin and Hard-cheese Salad

Serves 2

*Gherkins, 50 g (2 oz)
finely sliced*

*Canned sweetcorn, 225 g
(8 oz) drained*

*Chinese leaf, 100 g (4 oz)
shredded*

*White radish (mooli),
100 g (4 oz) slivered*

*Hard cheese, 50 g (2 oz)
cut into tiny cubes*

*Fresh coriander leaves to
garnish*

For the dressing
Dark sesame oil, 3 tbs

Soy sauce, 1 tbs

*A little grated fresh root
ginger, to taste*

*Raspberry vinegar (see
p. 121), 2 tsp*

Sugar, 1 tsp

1 clove of garlic, crushed

Combine all the prepared salad ingredients and toss in the dressing. Serve garnished with coriander leaves.

To prepare the dressing, stir all the ingredients together and allow to stand for at least half an hour before using, so that all the flavours can permeate.

Cucumber in Mustard Dressing

Serves 2

Sesame seeds, 1 tbs

Vinegar, 1 tsp

Soy sauce, 1 tsp

Sugar, 1 tsp

Dijon mustard, 2 tsp

Olive oil, 2 tbs

*1 large cucumber, peeled,
cut lengthwise and de-seeded*

Brown the sesame seeds under the grill. Crush them in a mortar and combine with the vinegar, soy sauce, sugar and mustard, mixing well to a smooth paste. Stir in the oil slowly, to make a thick dressing.

Slice the cucumber halves very thinly and combine with the sauce. Chill for an hour before using. Toss again just before serving.

Pasta Salad Special

Serves 2–3

*Small courgettes, 75 g
(3 oz) thinly sliced*

*Celeriac, 75 g (3 oz)
peeled and grated*

*½ a yellow pepper,
de-seeded and diced*

*Mange-tout, 50 g (2 oz)
finely sliced diagonally*

*French beans, 50 g (2 oz)
steamed and cut into short
lengths*

Chopped dill, 1 tbs

*1 large clove of garlic,
crushed*

Olive oil, 150 ml (¼ pint)

*Pasta quills, 175 g (6 oz)
cooked 'al dente'*

Salt and pepper

Mix all the prepared vegetables together
in a bowl with the dill. Stir the garlic into
the olive oil and toss the pasta quills in it,
then toss in the vegetables and mix well.
Season to taste with salt and pepper, and
leave in a cool place for several hours
before serving, tossing from time to time
so that the pasta absorbs all the oil.

Dilled Green-bean Salad

Serves 2

*French beans, 100 g
(4 oz) trimmed*

1 clove of garlic, crushed

6 sprigs of dill

¼ tsp dill seeds

A few mustard seeds

Sugar, 2 tbs

*Cider vinegar, 100 ml
(4 fl. oz)*

Salt, 1 tbs

Steam the beans until tender but still
crisp – 3–4 minutes. Cool and put them
in the bottom of a glass dish. Add the
crushed garlic, dill sprigs and seeds, and
mustard seeds. In a saucepan combine
the sugar, vinegar, salt and a little water,
and bring to the boil. Pour the mixture
over the beans and leave to cool. Chill it
overnight, covered.

Nasturtium Salad

Serves 2–3

10 nasturtium flowers

½ a radicchio lettuce, shredded

Small crisp lettuce, washed

10 sprigs of parsley

6 black olives, stoned

3 tomatoes, cut into wedges

4 spring onions, slivered

½ a ripe avocado, diced

Vinaigrette, 5 tbs

Put the prepared ingredients into a large salad bowl, reserving four of the flowers. Toss in the vinaigrette, then decorate the salad with the remaining flowers.

Goat's Cheese Salad

Serves 2

Handful each of curly endive lettuce leaves and oak leaf lettuce leaves

Raspberry vinaigrette (see p. 121)

Crème fraîche, 100 g (4 oz)

Goat's cheese, 175 g (6 oz) cut into 8 slices

8 thin slices of French bread

Fennel, thyme and marjoram, 2 tbs chopped

Salt

Trim and wash the lettuce leaves and dry them. Toss in a raspberry vinaigrette. Arrange on two plates and sprinkle with a little of the chopped herbs.

Put the crème fraîche into a saucepan and reduce it by half over a vigorous heat with a little salt and a pinch or two of finely chopped herbs.

Place each slice of cheese on a slice of French bread and place in a very hot oven (240°C/475°F/gas 9) for 5 minutes.

Arrange half of the slices on each plate and serve the reduced crème fraîche separately as a sauce.

Winter Slaw

Serves 3–4

*White cabbage, 225 g
(8 oz) shredded*

*Brussels sprouts, 75 g (3 oz)
trimmed and thinly sliced*

*White radish (mooli),
50 g (2 oz) grated*

1 large carrot, grated

*Celeriac, 75 g (3 oz)
peeled and coarsely grated*

Sunflower seeds, 3 tbs

*Mayonnaise (garlic
mayonnaise if preferred),
5 tbs*

Mix all the prepared ingredients together and toss thoroughly in the mayonnaise. Serve with granary bread.

Caroline's Salad

Serves 2

*1 oak-leaf lettuce, washed
and trimmed*

*Alfalfa sprouts, 50 g
(2 oz)*

*Sunflower seeds, 1 tbs
browned under the grill*

Small bunch of basil leaves

For the dressing
*Fresh-pressed orange juice,
3 tbs*

*Blackcurrant cordial (such
as Ribena), 1 tbs*

Dark sesame oil, 2 tbs

Put the salad ingredients into a bowl. Stir the three dressing ingredients together and toss the salad in the dressing thoroughly just before serving.

Mixed Vegetable Salad Sweet and Sour

Serves 3–4

Red cabbage, 175 g (6 oz) shredded

French beans, 75 g (3 oz) cooked

Jerusalem artichokes, 175 g (6 oz) peeled, cooked and diced

Canned sweetcorn, 75 g (3 oz) drained

Sweet and sour dressing

1 clove of garlic

½ a small onion, finely sliced

Honey, 2 tbs

Tarragon vinegar, 3 tbs

Lemon juice, 2 tbs

Mustard, 1 tsp

Snipped chives, 1 tsp

Snipped dill, 1 tsp
Parsley, 1 tsp finely chopped

Vegetable oil, 150 ml (¼ pint)

Salt to taste

To prepare the dressing, put the garlic, onion, honey and vinegar into the blender. Add the lemon juice and mustard, and salt to taste. With the blade working, add the oil in a thin stream and blend the dressing until it thickens. Put it into a jar and leave it to stand overnight for the flavours to amalgamate. Strain the dressing into a jug, and stir in the chives, dill and parsley.

Arrange the shredded cabbage in the centre of a serving-platter and toss it in half of the dressing. Arrange the French beans, artichokes and corn decoratively around the cabbage. Serve the remaining dressing in a sauceboat.

Turnip and Carrot Slaw

Serves 2–3

Raw turnip, 100 g (4 oz) grated

Carrots, 100 g (4 oz) grated

Vinaigrette, 4 tbs

Snipped dill, 2 tbs

Soft-leaved lettuce

Salt and freshly ground pepper

In a bowl combine the grated turnips and carrots and dress with the vinaigrette. Toss well, then add the dill and season to taste with salt and pepper. Arrange on salad plates lined with the lettuce.

Cauliflower and Hazelnut Salad

Serves 2

½ a medium cauliflower, cut into florets

Hazelnuts, 25 g (1 oz) coarsely chopped

Small bunch of watercress, washed and trimmed

Gruyère, 25 g (1 oz) cut into tiny cubes

Vinaigrette, 2 tbs

1 clove of garlic, crushed (optional)

Croûtons to garnish (see p. 37)

Steam the cauliflower florets until just tender but still slightly crisp. Cool, then mix with the chopped nuts, watercress and cubed cheese. Toss in the vinaigrette with the garlic if desired. Chill, and serve garnished with egg-roll slices.

Swiss Cheese and Cabbage Slaw

Serves 2–3

Cabbage, 225 g (8 oz) finely shredded

Swiss cheese, 100 g (4 oz) grated

Green pepper, 50 g (2 oz) seeded and finely chopped

½ a small onion, finely chopped

Celery seeds, 1 tsp

Mayonnaise, 5 tbs

Salt, pepper and Tabasco

Combine the cabbage, grated cheese, pepper, onion and celery seeds and stir in the mayonnaise. Season to taste with salt, pepper and a little Tabasco.

Courgette Salad

Serves 2–3

Courgettes, 350 g (12 oz)
grated

Salt, 1 tsp

Plain yogurt, 2 tbs

Mayonnaise, 2 tbs

Dijon mustard, 1 tbs

1 clove of garlic, crushed

1 soft-leaved lettuce

Tomato quarters to garnish

Toss the grated courgettes with the salt and let them stand, covered, for at least 1 hour. Press all the moisture out with the back of a wooden spoon, and dry on paper towels. In another bowl combine the yogurt, mayonnaise, mustard and garlic. Add the courgettes and mix thoroughly. Chill the salad for at least 30 minutes and serve it on a bed of lettuce, garnished with the tomato quarters.

Feta and Celery Salad

Serves 2

Feta, 175 g (6 oz)
crumbled

3 stalks of celery, thinly
sliced

1 canned pimento, chopped
small

Fresh thyme or oregano,
2 tbs chopped

Vinaigrette, 2 tbs

1 oak-leaf lettuce, washed
and trimmed

Mix the feta with the celery, pimento and chopped herbs. Dress with vinaigrette. Place the lettuce leaves on two separate plates, and spoon half of the feta and celery salad in the centre of each one.

Tomatoes al Pesto

Serves 2

1 small lettuce

Vinaigrette, 2 tbs

Pesto (see p. 120), 3 tbs

1 large tomato, sliced

Fresh basil leaves to garnish

Toss the inner lettuce leaves in the vinaigrette and put 3–4 leaves on each plate. Spread some pesto on to each slice of tomato and place on top of the lettuce leaves. Garnish with fresh basil leaves and serve.

Vegetable Salad Malay-style

Serves 2

Beansprouts, 50 g (2 oz)

French beans, 100 g (4 oz) steamed until tender

Small new potatoes, 100 g (4 oz) boiled in their skins and quartered

Courgettes, 100 g (4 oz) sliced and steamed until just tender

Chinese leaf, 50 g (2 oz) shredded

1 small crisp lettuce, shredded

1 hard-boiled egg, quartered

For the dressing

Fresh root ginger, 1 cm (½ inch)

1 clove of garlic, crushed

½ a fresh chilli, seeds removed

½ a small onion, chopped

Sesame oil, 2 tbs

Dry-roasted peanuts, 100 g (4 oz) ground

Salt

Juice of ½ a lemon

Coconut milk (see p. 54), 150 ml (¼ pint)

Mix all the prepared salad ingredients together in a salad bowl.

To make the dressing, mince the ginger, garlic, chilli and onion in the blender, and then stir in the rest of the ingredients. Simmer until the sauce is thick. Cool, then dress the salad with the mixture.

DESSERTS

Peach and Yogurt Melba

Serves 2

2 ripe peaches
Juice of ½ an orange
Greek yogurt, 175 g
(6 oz)
A few fresh or frozen
raspberries

Ripe peaches are marinated in fresh orange juice, which is then mixed with a yogurt topping. A light dessert, simple to prepare and refreshing on the palate.

Cover the peaches with boiling water and leave for a minute. Peel the skins off the fruit, using a sharp knife. Stone and slice them and put them into a bowl. Pour the orange juice over them and leave to marinate, turning from time to time, for 30 minutes.

Lift the slices out of the juice and place in the bottom of two glass dishes. Mix the juice with the yogurt and spoon over the fruit. Decorate with a few raspberries and it is ready to serve.

Bittersweet Temptation

Serves 2

Crème fraîche, 175 g
(6 oz)

Orange marmalade, 1 tbs

Whisky (optional)

Icing sugar

The unusual flavour of orange marmalade balances the fresh creaminess of crème fraîche, heightened if you like with a little whisky. The dessert is frozen lightly just before serving – and it is temptation indeed.

Whisk the crème fraîche and stir in the marmalade. Lace with a little whisky, to taste, if desired. Put into two little dishes and freeze lightly – about 1 hour. Sprinkle with a little icing sugar before serving.

Pears with Bilberries

Serves 2

2 large pears, peeled and
left whole

Butter, 25 g (1 oz) cut
into small pieces

1 glass of red wine

Caster sugar, 40 g
(1½ oz)

Cinnamon stick, 2.5 cm
(1 inch)

Bilberries (or blueberries),
100 g (4 oz)

Crème fraîche to serve

Poaching pears in a slow oven transforms them completely, and although cooked through until soft, they do not lose their firm, grainy texture. A little cinnamon and red wine flavour the sauce, and the bilberries are an inspired touch.

Arrange the pears in an ovenproof dish. Add the butter, red wine, sugar, cinnamon stick and bilberries or blueberries.

Bake at 200°C/400°F/gas 6 for 1 hour, covered with foil and basting every 10 minutes. Serve hot or warm, with crème fraîche.

Gooseberry Compôte

Serves 2

Sugar, 50 g (2 oz)

Water, 150 ml (¼ pint)

Gooseberries, 225 g (8 oz)

Vanilla stick, 5 cm
(2 inch)

Crème fraîche or Greek
yogurt to serve

Make this dessert in early summer when gooseberries come into season – one of the most lovely of our soft fruits. Gooseberries make gorgeous pies and crumbles too – but this recipe, for all its simplicity, brings out the best in them.

Dissolve the sugar in the water with the vanilla stick, stirring, and boil for 5 minutes until it is syrupy. Add the gooseberries to the syrup and poach very gently for 10 minutes. Cool. Serve chilled, in two glass dishes, with crème fraîche or Greek yogurt.

Strawberry Cocktail

Serves 2

Fresh orange juice, 4 tbs

Caster sugar, 1 tbs

2 sprigs of fresh mint

Strawberries, 175 g (6 oz)
washed and hulled

Lemon syllabub (see
p. 113), 150 ml (¼ pint)

Mint to decorate

Strawberries are marinated in a mixture of orange juice and mint, and just before serving are topped with a home-made lemon syllabub. A summer dessert with a difference.

Mix the orange juice with the sugar and mint and leave to stand for 1 hour. Cut the strawberries into thin strips and add them to the juice mixture. Leave to stand for a further 10 minutes.

Just before serving, divide the strawberries, and their juices, between two glass serving-dishes. Cover with the chilled lemon syllabub and decorate with a sprig of mint.

Scarlet Fruit Salad

Serves 2–3

Red wine, 50 ml (2 fl. oz)

Caster sugar, 25 g (1 oz)

Redcurrants, 75 g (3 oz)
topped and tailed

Raspberries, 75 g (3 oz)
hulled

Cherries, 175 g (6 oz)
washed and stoned

Crème fraîche to serve

This red fruit salad looks quite spectacular, and its flavours live up to its looks. A lovely dessert for fine summer weather and for eating *al fresco*.

Heat the wine with the sugar until the sugar dissolves. Bring to the boil and pour over the fruit in a bowl. Allow the fruit salad to stand at room temperature for an hour or two, stirring from time to time. Chill, and serve with crème fraîche.

Chocolate Biscuit Cake

Serves 4

Butter or margarine, cocoa,
biscuit crumbs, sugar,
100 g (4 oz) each

1 egg

Petit Beurre or Osborne
biscuits, 100 g (4 oz)
broken into bite-sized
pieces

Crème fraîche to serve

A firm favourite over the years, this cake proves ever-popular. Delightfully simple to prepare — no cooking! — it makes a lovely dessert at any time of the year, and especially for picnics.

Work the butter or margarine with the cocoa, and mix in the biscuit crumbs. Mix the sugar with a little water and dissolve it over a low heat, stirring. Then bring to the boil and simmer until syrupy — about 3–4 minutes. Blend into the cocoa mixture. Stir in the egg, then fold in the biscuits broken into bite-sized pieces. Put into an oiled loaf tin and chill until set. Turn out when completely cold and serve sliced, with crème fraîche.

Figs with Orange

Serves 2–3

Orange juice, 75 ml
(3 fl. oz)

Brown sugar, 1 tbs

1 cinnamon stick

2 cloves

Dried figs, 150 g (5 oz)

Lemon juice, 1 tbs

1 large orange, peeled and
cut into segments

Thick Greek yogurt, 100 g
(4 oz)

Clear honey, 1 tbs

This is a wonderful way to use dried figs, poaching them in an orange syrup and then adding fresh orange segments. You can make this dessert at any time of the year, served with a delicious mixture of Greek yogurt and honey.

Put the orange juice and sugar into a pan with the spices and heat gently until the sugar dissolves. Add the figs and lemon juice, and put in enough water to just cover the fruit. Cover the pan and simmer gently for 5 minutes. Remove the figs and boil the syrup hard until it reduces. Pour over the figs, add the orange segments, and chill. Just before serving, stir the honey into the Greek yogurt and pass it around to spoon over the fig dish.

Melon in Lime Syrup

Serves 2

1 ogen or Charentais melon
Water, 150 ml (¼ pint)
Sugar, 75 g (3 oz)
Juice and finely grated rinds
of 2 limes

Chilled melon in a lime syrup makes an elegant sweet course, served with crème fraîche or thick set yogurt. Light, fresh, summery food.

Cut the melon in half and discard the seeds. Cut out the flesh with a melon baller. Put the water and sugar into a pan and bring to the boil, stirring until the sugar dissolves. Boil hard to a thick syrup, and then dilute with the lime juice. Add the rind, then pour over the melon balls and leave for 1 hour at room temperature. Chill thoroughly before serving.

Apricot Delight

Serves 2

Dried apricots, preferably
unsulphured, 50 g (2 oz)
Greek yogurt, 175 g
(6 oz)
1 egg white, stiffly beaten
Grated chocolate to
decorate

This recipe is a long-established favourite and can be made at any time of the year. If you make it with unsulphured dried apricots the result will be noticeably more delicious.

Soak the apricots in water for just 1 hour, then chop them roughly. They will be slightly crunchy. Fold them into the yogurt and mix well. Fold the stiffly beaten egg white into the mixture and spoon into two dishes. Sprinkle with grated chocolate. Serve as soon as possible.

Greek Yogurt Syllabub

Serves 2–3

Greek yogurt, 225 g (8 oz)

Brandy or lemon juice, 2 tbs

3 pieces stem ginger, chopped

Syrup from the jar, 1 tbs

Icing sugar

Fresh peach slices to garnish

For those who love stem ginger, this is a real treat: a lemon-flavoured base of thick Greek yogurt for the ginger, topped with a garnish of fresh peaches. Scrumptious.

Whisk the yogurt and stir in the brandy or lemon juice. Fold in the chopped ginger and syrup, and sweeten to taste if necessary. Spoon into two or three serving-glasses. Chill thoroughly for at least 4 hours, or overnight.

Serve garnished with fresh peach slices.

White-chocolate Mousse

Serves 2–3

White chocolate, 75 g (3 oz) finely grated

Thick set yogurt, 3 tbs

1 egg, separated

Icing sugar, 15 g (½ oz)

White chocolate imparts a very delicate flavour to a mousse, and this dessert has a velvety, slightly grainy texture on the palate. Lovely after a salad meal.

Stir the grated white chocolate into the yogurt. Beat the egg yolk and stir in. Beat the egg white until stiff, then fold in the icing sugar and beat again until very stiff. Fold into the white-chocolate mixture and put into a glass serving-bowl. Chill for 2 hours, then serve.

Lemon Syllabub

Serves 2

Lemon juice, 5 tbs

Lemon rind, 1 tbs grated

Caster sugar, 2 tbs

White wine (optional), 1 tbs

Thick Greek yogurt, 225 g (8 oz), or cream, 300 ml (½ pt)

Very light and fresh, this is a wonderful way of treating yogurt or cream. Simplicity itself, yet a transformation. Serve it with delicate biscuits of your choice and it is a feast.

Combine the lemon juice, rind and sugar, and the wine if desired. Chill the mixture until it is very cold. Strain and beat into the yogurt or cream until completely amalgamated. Spoon into tall glasses and chill.

Coffee Mousse

Serves 2

2 egg yolks

Icing sugar, 25 g (1 oz)

Very strong black coffee, 2 tbs

White chocolate, 100 g (4 oz) grated

Double cream, 150 ml (¼ pint)

This unusual coffee mousse is made with white chocolate, very finely grated, which gives it a grainy texture. A rich dessert, best eaten after a light salad meal.

Beat the egg yolks with the sugar, until light and creamy, then add the coffee. Stir in the grated white chocolate. Beat the cream until thick and fold into the mixture. Spoon into two glass dishes and chill for at least 4 hours.

Pots au Chocolat

Serves 3

Dark chocolate, 50 g (2 oz)

Double cream, 75 ml (3 fl. oz)

Milk, 100 ml (4 fl. oz) plus 2 tbs

Sugar, 4 tbs

Instant coffee powder, 1 tsp

2 large egg yolks

1 whole egg

This recipe is a hit. Dark, velvety chocolate pots that melt in the mouth and flavours that linger on the palate. Truly delicious.

Melt the chocolate in a bowl set over simmering water. In a heavy saucepan combine the cream, milk and 2 tbs of the sugar. Bring to the boil, stirring. In a small bowl combine 2 tbs of milk with the coffee powder and stir into the milk mixture with the chocolate.

Beat the egg yolks with a whole egg and the remaining sugar until well blended. Add the milk mixture in a stream, whisking all the time. Pour into three ramekin dishes and set in a pan of water. Cover with foil and bake at 170°C/325°F/gas 3 for 20–25 minutes or until just set. Remove and cool for 5 minutes. Uncover and cool completely. Chill for at least 3 hours or overnight. Garnish with a dollop of cream just before serving.

Hazelnut Mousse

Serves 2

2 egg yolks

Sugar, 50 g (2 oz)

*Unsalted butter, 25 g
(1 oz) melted*

Strong black coffee, 2 tbs

*Hazelnuts, 100 g (4 oz)
toasted and ground*

*Crème fraîche, 100 g
(4 oz)*

A classic hazelnut mousse makes a delightful dessert for special occasions. This one is flavoured with some black coffee – two sophisticated flavours in one dish.

Beat the egg yolks until they are pale, add the sugar and beat until the mixture is thick. Beat in the melted butter and stir in the coffee and the ground hazelnuts. Whisk the crème fraîche and fold into the nut mixture gently but thoroughly. Chill for at least 2 hours before serving.

Key Lime Pie

Serves 4

Biscuit crust
*Digestive biscuits, 175 g
(6 oz)*

Caster sugar, 2 tbs

*Butter or margarine, 75 g
(3 oz) melted*

For the filling
3 egg yolks, beaten

*Canned condensed milk,
400 g (14 oz)*

*Lime juice, 100 ml
(4 fl. oz)*

Lime rind, 1 tbs grated

Whipped cream to serve

Exquisitely sinful, this scrumptious pie is not for waistline-watchers, nor for those who are purists about diet. But for those who are able to throw caution to the winds, this is your reward!

Crush the biscuits to fine crumbs – use the blender for this if possible. Add the sugar to the crumbs, then mix well with the melted butter. Press into a greased 20 cm (8 inch) flan case and chill for at least 30 minutes.

To prepare the filling, first beat the egg yolks until pale and creamy. Slowly beat in the condensed milk. Stir the lime juice and rind into the mixture. Pour on to the biscuit base and freeze. Remove from the freezer when well frozen and spread with whipped cream. Eat straight away, without defrosting – it does not freeze hard and is delectable chilled in this way.

Orange Syllabub Trifle

Serves 3–4

For the orange syllabub

Finely grated peel and juice of 1 orange

Caster sugar, 50 g (2 oz)

Crème fraîche, 175 g (6 oz)

Thick yogurt, 225 g (8 oz)

For the trifle

4 trifle cakes

Orange juice, 150 ml (¼ pint)

8 segments of peeled orange and a small sprig of fresh mint to garnish

A light, simple trifle: a layer of cake is soaked with fresh orange juice, then topped with a mouth-watering layer of crème fraîche and yogurt flavoured with orange rind and juice. Orange segments decorate the edge of this lovely dessert.

Put the peel and orange juice into a bowl with the sugar. Leave to marinate. Strain the liquid into a clean bowl and add the crème fraîche gradually, beating until thick. Fold in the yogurt. Chill for a few hours or overnight.

Cut the trifle sponges in half lengthwise. Lay them in the bottom of a small serving-dish, moisten with the orange juice, and finish with a layer of the syllabub. Place segments of orange around the edge. Chill for 2–3 hours before serving. Decorate with a small sprig of mint.

Bombe Favorite

Serves 2–3

Crème fraîche, 175 g (6 oz)

Icing sugar, 15 g (½ oz) plus 2 tbs sifted

Little macaroons, 75 g (3 oz) broken in pieces

1 egg white

A favourite indeed. Small pieces of macaroon are folded into a crème fraîche ice cream base and lightly frozen. A delicious dessert for summer.

Whisk the crème fraîche with the sifted icing sugar. Fold in the macaroon pieces. Beat the egg white until very stiff, add 2 tbs of icing sugar and beat again. Fold into the crème fraîche mixture and put into a serving-dish. Freeze lightly – about 2 hours – before serving, so that it comes out like soft ice cream.

Chocolate Terrine

Serves 4

Dark chocolate, 100 g
(4 oz)

Butter, 100 g (4 oz)

Caster sugar, 40 g
(1½ oz)

2 eggs, beaten

Plain flour, 25 g (1 oz)

Crème fraîche to serve

A slim, dark slice of velvety chocolate on your plate, a dollop of crème fraîche – what could be better? This is a light yet rich dessert, irresistible to chocolate-lovers.

Melt the chocolate with the butter and sugar over a bowl of hot water. Beat the eggs and stir in the flour. Stir the two mixtures together and pour into a greased loaf tin lined with greaseproof paper. Bake at 200°C/400°F/gas 6 for 45 minutes or until a knife comes out clean from the centre. Cool on a rack and turn out when cold. Serve sliced thinly, with crème fraîche.

Maggie's Apricot Cream

Serves 2–3

Canned apricots, 175 g
(6 oz) drained

Soya milk, 300 ml
(½ pint)

This unlikely dessert is simplicity and economy incarnate. Looking at the recipe it is hard to believe – but it works. The soya milk turns to a set cream overnight, and it looks as if you have spent hours preparing what probably took 3 minutes. A cooling sweet course, with lovely textures.

Slice the canned apricots and put them into the bottom of a serving-dish. Pour the milk over them and chill overnight. The soya milk will set to a light cream, and the natural sugars in the fruit are sufficient sweetness. Lovely textures!

SAUCES AND DRESSINGS

Béchamel Sauce

*Butter or sunflower
margarine, 40 g (1½ oz)*

Plain flour, 2 tbs

*Hot milk, 300 ml
(½ pint)*

*Salt, pepper and a pinch
of ground nutmeg*

Melt the butter or margarine in a heavy saucepan. Gradually stir in the flour with a wooden spoon over a low heat, and then add the milk slowly, stirring constantly until the sauce thickens. Season to taste with salt, pepper and ground nutmeg, and simmer gently over a very low heat for 5 minutes before using.

Mustard and Cheese Sauce

*Béchamel sauce (see above),
450 ml (¾ pint)*

*Moutarde de Meaux,
1½ tbs*

*Cheddar or Gruyère, 50 g
(2 oz) grated*

Salt and pepper

*Single cream to finish
(optional)*

Gently heat the béchamel sauce in a heavy pan and stir in the mustard. When well combined, add the cheese and heat until melted. Add salt and pepper to taste. Finish with the cream if so desired.

Mushroom Sauce

*Béchamel sauce (see
p. 119), 300 ml
(½ pint)*

*Large buttom mushrooms,
225 g (8 oz)*

Salt and pepper

Heat the béchamel gently, stirring so that
it remains smooth. Mince the mushrooms
in the food processor and stir them into the
sauce. Simmer very gently for 5 minutes.
Season to taste with salt and pepper.

Sesame Sauce

Sesame oil, 5 tbs

Wine vinegar, 1 tbs

Soy sauce, 2 tbs

*2 spring onions, trimmed
and finely chopped*

*Sesame seeds, 1 tbs browned
lightly under the grill*

Stir the sesame oil, wine vinegar and soy
sauce together until well mixed. Add the
spring onions and sesame seeds. Dress
either hot or warm pasta with the sauce.

Pesto

1 large bunch fresh basil

*2 large cloves of garlic,
peeled and crushed*

Pine nuts, 75 g (3 oz)

*Parmesan cheese, 50 g
(2 oz) finely grated*

*Olive oil, 150 ml
(¼ pint)*

Salt to taste (optional)

Put all the ingredients into the food-
processor or liquidizer and blend until
smooth. Season to taste with salt if necessary. Store in an airtight jar in the refrigerator, where it will keep for several weeks.

Raspberry Vinegar

*Raspberries, 650 g
(1½ lb)*

*Malt vinegar, 1.2 litres
(2 pints)*

Sugar, 900 g (2 lb)

Cover the raspberries with water in a large pan, and simmer for 20 minutes. Strain off the juice – there will be about 1.2 litres (2 pints). Add the vinegar and the sugar and stir over a gentle heat. Bring to the boil and simmer for 15–20 minutes, until the liquid becomes syrupy and clings to a spoon. Decant into clean glass bottles and cork. Store in a cool, dark place where it will keep indefinitely.

Raspberry Vinaigrette

*Raspberry vinegar (see
above), 1 tbs*

Mild mustard, 1 tsp

Olive oil, 50 ml (2 fl.oz)

Salt and pepper

Mix the raspberry vinegar into the mustard and season with salt and pepper. Stir in the olive oil gradually, until the dressing amalgamates.

Orange Vinaigrette

Fresh orange juice, 2 tbs

Mild mustard, 1 tsp

*Olive oil, 100 ml
(4 fl. oz)*

Salt and pepper

Mix the orange juice into the mustard and season with salt and pepper. Stir in the olive oil gradually, stirring thoroughly all the time, until the mixture amalgamates. Leave to stand for a while before using, to allow the flavours to blend.

Mayonnaise

1 free-range egg
Dry mustard, 1 tsp
Salt and pepper
Sunflower or olive oil,
300 ml (½ pint)

Break the egg into the blender and add the mustard, salt and pepper. Liquidize, and then as the machine is running pour in a thin stream of oil. Stop pouring from time to time to avoid the possibility of the mayonnaise curdling and allowing it to thicken.

Check the seasoning and store in an airtight jar in the refrigerator.

Garlic Mayonnaise

Ingredients as above plus
garlic to taste

Crush the amount of garlic you require into the mayonnaise above, or into a commercial brand, about 30 minutes before serving. It is best eaten within 24 hours, because the garlic may turn slightly rancid after a longer period.

Garlic Vinaigrette

Tarragon vinegar, 1 tbs
Mild mustard, 1 tsp
Olive oil, 100 ml (4 fl. oz)
Garlic, 2 medium cloves
crushed
Salt and pepper

Mix the tarragon vinegar with the mustard, gradually pour in the oil, stirring all the time so it thickens. Season with a little salt and pepper, then stir in the crushed garlic. Leave to stand for 20–30 minutes before serving.

Lemon Mustard Dressing

Lemon juice, 4 tbs

1 clove of garlic, crushed

Sugar, 2 tsp

Dijon mustard, 2 tsp

*Olive or sunflower oil,
100 ml (4 fl. oz)*

Salt and pepper

Put the lemon juice into a bowl and stir in the garlic, sugar and mustard. Gradually stir in the oil until it begins to thicken and carry on stirring until the dressing amalgamates. Season to taste with salt and pepper and leave to stand for a little while before using.

Yogurt Dressing

*Vinaigrette, 150 ml
(¼ pint)*

*Natural thick set yogurt,
100 ml (4 fl. oz)*

Stir the vinaigrette into the yogurt until smooth and creamy. That's all. Delicious on a fresh tomato salad and with coleslaw.

Raspberry Soy Dressing

*Raspberry vinegar (see
p. 121), 5 tbs*

Soy sauce, 2 tbs

*Crushed garlic to taste
(optional)*

Mix the raspberry vinegar with the soy sauce and add the garlic to taste if wanted. Leave to stand for a while before serving to allow the flavours to mingle. A lovely summer dressing for leafy salads.

Basic Crêpe Recipe

For 6 pancakes
Plain flour, 65 g
(2½ oz)

1 large egg

Milk, 150 ml (¼ pint)

Water, 75 ml (3 fl. oz)

Vegetable oil, 1 tsp

Pinch of salt

Put all the ingredients into the liquidizer
and blend for 1 minute. Leave to stand in
a cool place for 2–3 hours.

INDEX